On Top of DENVER the World

URBAN
TAPESTRY
SERIES
TOWERY
PUBLISHING, INC.

Denver: On Top of the World

Introduction by **Pete Smythe**

Art Direction by **Brian Groppe**

Contents

6

Introduction

Pete Smythe's introductory letter captures the essence of Denver, reflecting on the qualities that make the city great.

11

Essay

Although the exquisite beauty of the city often defies description, Denver and its inhabitants have never ceased to inspire our efforts to capture them in words.

20

Photo-Essay

An enduring portrait of Denver featuring images from the area's finest photographers.

164
Profiles in Excellence
A look at the corporations, businesses, professional groups, and community service organizations that have made this book possible.

252
Photographers

256
Index of Profiles

◆ © ERIC WUNROW

This book is dedicated to the memory of Pete Smythe.

People who know me as the mayor of East Tin Cup, Colorado, may think it's ironic that I was asked to write this introduction about the big city of Denver. After all, I've devoted a good deal of my adult life to serving East Tin Cup, which is so small that we need neither taxes nor parking meters to make life complicated for us.

East Tin Cup is a place of Old West values, small-town neighborliness, good humor, good will, and free hay for the horses. It's a place of imagination and magic.

To tell the truth, East Tin Cup is something that some buddies and I dreamed up over 40 years ago, our off-kilter notion of what an Old West town ought to be, where the codes of honor, individuality, and freedom still are cherished.

In reality, Denver is the true result of those dreams, those codes, those freedoms. It's the culmination of an old way of life that still exists and is always new. Even though Denver has become big and fast and modern, it's still the true heart of the Old West.

Denver has always been the city I love to call home. Throughout my career as a musician, a writer, a radio announcer, and a TV show host (among other occupations), I have found here the people and the beliefs—the way of life—that have made me love this city.

Sure, there were a couple of brief stints back in the 1930s and 1940s when I tried living in Los Angeles. I worked as a singing waiter, although I recall spending a good deal more time singing in the kitchen in my role as dishwasher than I did out in the dining room. Later, I was fortunate enough to work with some of the era's biggest stars when I got a job in radio out there. But in another twist of irony, I eventually had to travel east to get back to the West, back to my home, back to Denver.

For those of you who are lifelong Denver residents, and for those of you who are new to the area, all I can tell you is that there is a mother lode of pleasure to be found here. Everything you could want out of life is right here, in the shadow of the majestic Rockies, waiting to be discovered.

East Tin Cup? That was a dream, a fantasy, a lark. But it's still out there, waiting for us. It's the place where imagination, dreams, and the creative spirit go to mingle with the iron-clad traditions of honesty, hard work, and discipline.

And its real name is Denver. Look for it, all over town, and you'll see it. Look for it in the neighborhoods, in the skyscrapers downtown, in the sprawling suburbs, and you'll find it. Because East Tin Cup always was Denver, and vice versa, the home of all that we cherish.

I just hope you find it as rewarding a place to live as I have.

Sincerely,
Pete Smythe

Few things are as inspiring as the view of the Front Range of the Rocky Mountains. You catch your first glimpse of the Rockies, coming from the New York side of the country, just as you enter Colorado from the plains state of Kansas, and they hover like a mirage—seeming to appear just above the horizon—shimmering like a magical apparition.

Yet, as inspiring as this long-distance view of the Rockies may be, actually living with the Front Range in your front yard is an existence second to none. Denver is located on high, rolling plains, but its mountain mystique begins in the nearby Foothills, a gentle series of peaks soaring to heights of 14,000 feet, known locally as the Front Range. The city is a beautiful portal to the Continental Divide.

Lest this begin to sound more like a description of Shangri-la than of a modern, urbane, cultured American metropolis, consider this: Denver's some 2 million metro population is within a day's drive (often less) of 11 national forests, a couple of dozen national parks and monuments, and 40 state parks—boasting millions of acres of forests, streams, mountains, and meadows. There are, according to the geographers, no fewer than 54 mountains with elevations of at least 14,000 feet near Denver, and the state of Colorado has, in all, more than a thousand mountains that tower more than 10,000 feet.

It is a magical apparition made real.

But, this is no airy outpost, either. Denver is the state capital. It has a history as both a gritty western trading center and a gold rush mecca, a place where fortunes have been made and lost and made again within the space of a very few years, where the cultural and artistic legacy of the pioneers has evolved into one of the country's most vibrant scenes. Every form of artistic expression, from the down-home to the highbrow, enjoys ample display in Denver, a city with a number of outstanding performing and visual arts venues.

What's more, Denver is a solid business center. Not confined to any one industry, the city has evolved into a diverse economic base with such sectors as tourism, real estate, health care, air transportation, education, information technologies, the military, telecommunications, livestock, and banking well represented in its economic mix.

It's also a sports lovers' town—the home of the two-time world champion Denver Broncos, Stanley Cup-winning Colorado Avalanche, Colorado Rockies baseball team, and Denver Nuggets NBA team. ☛

So, magical though it may seem from a distance, Denver is a living and breathing city, a great place to live or to work. Its residential areas are plentiful and, today, large suburbs add to the Denver metro area's diverse array of lifestyle options, making it one of the world's most interesting places to call home.

Apparently, interesting is how it has always been in Denver.

Although evidence of inhabitants dates back to 12,000 B.C., Denver (as we know it) was settled in 1859, during the Pike's Peak or Bust gold rush. With major strikes in the areas surrounding the city, Denver rose from several different mining settlements.

Three settlements, to be precise. They had sprung up in response to the first gold strike in 1858, and had each tried to claim dominance as the miners and prospectors streamed into town. The whole thing was settled, according to popular lore, in 1859 over a barrel of whiskey. Under the influence of its contents, the settlements—which were sprawling encampments of tents, for the most part, with a few log cabin structures here and there—decided to join forces, adopt the name of Denver, and call the animosity quits.

The newspaperman Horace Greeley's famous quote from that year sums up the look and feel of the new city nicely. Denver, he wrote, is a "log city of 150 dwellings, not three-fourths completed nor two-thirds inhabited, nor one-third fit to be."

From early on, it appeared that maybe this wasn't such a hot place for a city after all. It wasn't located on a major road. Or river. Or lake. It had no rail service. It was prone to floods so severe that even the Indians had warned the pioneers that this might not be such a great place for a permanent settlement. And for several months out of the year, the snowy weather

made the tents and muddy streets mighty uncomfortable, to say the least. About the only thing that Denver had going for it, at first, was a saloon, which just happened to be the first permanent structure in town. (Many locals insist that this fact alone tells you just about all you need to know of early Denver's character.)

Despite fires, Indian wars, and (yes) floods, Denver flourished so rapidly that even the old-timers were amazed. The University of Denver was founded in 1864—just five years after the tent city was founded—a sure sign that civilization had descended on the still-muddy frontier town. Gold strikes continued to bring prosperous entrepreneurs, along with scores of gold-hungry prospectors, all of whom carried with them their distinctive tastes and lifestyles.

A brief scare came in 1869 and 1870, as the vaunted Union Pacific transcontinental railway bypassed Denver in favor of a more northerly route that skirted the highest passes in the Rockies. Denver's business community, undaunted by such a potential setback, set out to build its own railroad to connect with the Union Pacific up in Cheyenne, and, in 1870, the railroad was completed. This not only ensured the city's survival, but led to a population explosion and economic boom that sent the city soaring from just fewer than 5,000 people when the railroad was finished to just more than 105,000 a mere 20 years later. Although silver had replaced gold as the most sought-after treasure in the area, Denver's golden years were definitely upon it.

And just as suddenly, it all seemed to come to a crashing halt. In 1893, the silver markets failed, causing banks to collapse and the city's silver barons to lose their fortunes as quickly as they had been amassed. Denver gravitated into other areas such as ranching and transportation, but only narrowly did it avoid a community meltdown. ☞

Although the city continued to gain in prominence—it is, after all, the state capital and the home of a branch of the U.S. Mint—it wasn't until after World War II that its fortunes once again began to soar in the way they had earlier. With the growth of suburbs such as Broomfield, Parker, Aurora, Englewood, Golden, Littleton, Louisville, and Boulder, the region's population has climbed to 2.3 million.

In 1995, Denver echoed its transportation success of 1870 when it opened Denver International Airport (DIA). This $4.3 billion facility covers 53 square miles and features five full-service runways that can accommodate some 120 planes an hour in good weather. This makes DIA one of the 10 busiest airports in the world. Noteworthy for its size alone, DIA is also gaining renown for its public art program—which features works by local and national artists created specifically for the airport—and its architecture, which features a multipeaked roof meant to mirror the jagged horizon of the nearby Rockies.

Whether it stands as evidence or catalyst, DIA has certainly played a role in Denver's latest population explosion: During the past 10 to 12 years, the metro population has grown by a whopping 23 percent, making this the 20th-largest metro area in America.

Boom years, apparently, are back. Once again, the world is learning just what a special place the city is.

Today's Denver enjoys a good many more monikers than Mile High City (although it is, still, proudly that). After some wrangling as to where, exactly, the city is a mile high, it was determined by some college engineering students in the 1960s that the State Capitol's 18th step works out to be exactly 5,280 feet above sea level. Or, a mile high.

Another nickname the city has earned is less widely known: America's skinniest city. According to a federal report, there are more thin people in Denver than anywhere else in America. (This, despite the city's claim to fame as the place where the

cheeseburger was invented in 1935 at a Humpty-Dumpty drive-in restaurant.) The report attributed the city's thinness to the active lifestyle, fine weather throughout most of the year, and relatively high level of educational achievement.

Others, though, swear that the reason has more to do with the city's elevation, and the "thin air" that people here breathe.

This city's altitude has a number of ramifications, most of which people don't even give much thought to. The obvious one is that newcomers need a day or two to get comfortable with the air's relatively low oxygen content. The lower water vapor makes for bluer skies and starrier nights. More home runs are hit at Coors Field due to baseballs traveling a reported 9 percent farther in the thin air. Water boils at a lower temperature (202 rather than 212 degrees), which requires adjustments for baking or even making a cup of tea..

And yet, there's beer, which brews up exceedingly well at this altitude. There is, most people are surprised to learn, more beer brewed in Denver than any other U.S. city. But, be careful if you're a newcomer and you drink it, since your oxygen-depleted blood makes the alcohol get right down on top of you. As always, moderation is called for.

What any of this—the elevation, the air, the beer—has to do with another of the city's recent claims to fame is even less clear. Denver is, according to many, the Baby Boomer Capital of America. It is home to a greater percentage—about 35 percent—of people between the ages of 35 and 54 than any other major U.S. metropolitan area. This, in turn, has meant that the city is experiencing a considerable "boomlet," resulting in a high proportion of school-age kids and challenging local schools to create facilities for them.

As if to answer, Denver has created one of the country's finest educational infrastructures, with excellent schools from pre-K to post-graduate.

Although it has more to do with the money the silver barons created more than 100 years ago than it does with the rare air, Denver has emerged as a first-rate cultural center as well. This was a city, after all, where folks in Levi's and muddy boots stood on sawdust floors beneath kerosene lamps to hear operas or watch Shakespeare. It's no wonder that modern-day Denver is one of the West's leading cultural centers.

Museums such as the Colorado History Museum, Black American West Museum, Denver Art Museum, and Denver Museum of Nature and Science are all leaders on a national level. The Denver Zoo, with some 4,000 animals, is one of the nation's best. The city's branch of the U.S. Mint produces more than 10 billion coins every year, and the building serves as one of the country's three largest holding facilities for gold bullion.

The Colorado State Capitol itself is both an artwork and a museum of sorts. Its dome is covered with pure gold (some 200 ounces in all), but the real treasure lies in the vantage of the whole stretch of the Front Range that is to be had from the rotunda, where plaques mark the huge mountains (such as Pikes Peak and Longs Peak) that you can see. It's one of the best places to experience the majesty of the Rockies, and a good way to learn just how immense this mountain range is. ☛

The Denver Center for Performing Arts features eight venues, for a combined total of some 10,00 seats, making it one of the largest such facilities in the country. Like Lincoln Center in New York, the arts complex has facilities for symphony concerts, dramatic offerings, dance, and Broadway-style productions.

But the real jewel in Denver's crown has always been its natural venue. The city's climate is milder and less wintry than most folks commonly think, thanks in large measure to the Continental Divide, which protects Denver from fierce weather patterns coming in from the northwest and Canada. Sure, it snows in the winter, but it can get hot in the summer, and there are four distinct seasons that are about equal in length. What's more, there are more sunny days in Denver than in Miami, and, since it's so far inland, the humidity that dogs much of the rest of the country is only rarely a factor here.

The result of this climate, along with the city's unique geography, is a natural wonder, a place to live that is nothing short of awesome. Sure, with more than 2 million residents, Denver suffers from a good many of the same problems shared by big cities everywhere.

But unlike cities everywhere, Denver has the mountains. While it's not a particularly hilly city—matter of fact, it's surprisingly flat, given its proximity to the Rockies—Denver is decidedly a mountain refuge. Sitting on the doorstep to the most majestic mountains in America, Denver's green lawns and tree-lined streets offer a perfect welcome mat, if you will, to the soaring Rockies that rise along the western horizon like an vision.

Here, the magic hinted at from the distant view rises to life, and one of the world's great cities beckons all who would come here to partake of it.

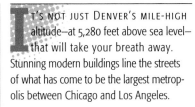

IT'S NOT JUST DENVER'S MILE-HIGH altitude—at 5,280 feet above sea level— that will take your breath away. Stunning modern buildings line the streets of what has come to be the largest metropolis between Chicago and Los Angeles.

ART AND ARCHITECTURE WALK HAND in hand along Denver's Fourteenth Avenue. The 540,000-square-foot Denver Central Public Library (RIGHT), designed by the renowned Michael Graves, opened its doors in 1995. Local architect George Hoover (OPPOSITE BOTTOM) created quite an opening of his own with his 1997 design of a new entrance for the Denver Art Museum (OPPOSITE TOP). The canopy opening between the library and the museum won awards, but few admirers.

AN ESTIMATED 220,000 NEW JOBS have been added to Denver's economy over the past 10 years, meaning significant growth and development for the city's business sector.

FROM ITS VANTAGE POINT EAST OF the Rocky Mountains, downtown Denver has become a hub of activity for the state. The three-level Colorado Convention Center (TOP) includes a contiguous exhibition space that stretches 292,000 square feet. For the best in live theater, locals turn to the Denver Center for the Performing Arts (BOTTOM), a four-block complex at Speer and Arapahoe. And just a short walk away, the Denver Pavilions (OPPOSITE) provides shopping, dining, and entertainment within its two-block section of the 16th Street Mall.

TRIVIAL PURSUIT: WHAT DO DENVER International Airport—or DIA—and New York have in common? The fabric roof of DIA features a catenary cable system that mirrors that of the Brooklyn Bridge. Opened in 1995 to much fanfare, the airport—which at 53 square miles is twice the size of Manhattan Island—handles more than 100,000 travelers daily in its dual-sided Elrey B. Jeppesen Terminal.

SIX COUNTIES FORM DENVER'S metropolitan area and, thanks to the region's expanding circle of freeways, traveling in and out of the city's core is a moving experience—with a few traffic jams thrown in for good measure.

UNION STATION

TRAVEL by TRAIN

UNION STATION

RAILYARD ALE

DENVER, CO.

High
Speed
Train
Approaching

ITS GLORY DAYS MAY BE BEHIND IT, BUT Denver's beaux arts Union Station still remains a regular stop for Amtrak's famous *California Zephyr*. Built in 1914 to replace the original 1880 depot destroyed in a fire, the facility features 64-foot-high ceilings and oak benches. These days, local mass transit revolves largely around light rail lines, which provide 14 miles of service.

CATCH, ANYBODY? THAT WAS THE question author Nick Hartshorn (OPPOSITE) put to people across the country for his 1997 book *Catch: A Discovery of America*. The Colorado native traveled 14,000 miles over four months to converse with the common folk during friendly games of pitch, chronicling their stories to share with readers. Denver fans can get their fill of the nation's pastime at beautiful Coors Field. Home to Major League Baseball's Colorado Rockies, the venue opened in 1995 in the city's Lower Downtown—or LoDo—district.

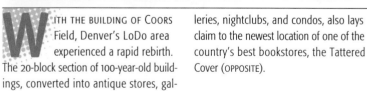

WITH THE BUILDING OF COORS Field, Denver's LoDo area experienced a rapid rebirth. The 20-block section of 100-year-old buildings, converted into antique stores, galleries, nightclubs, and condos, also lays claim to the newest location of one of the country's best bookstores, the Tattered Cover (OPPOSITE).

© CATHERINE GEHM

OCATED IN THE HEART OF DOWNTOWN Denver, a one-block stretch of Larimer—the city's oldest street—has become a shopping and entertainment mecca. Larimer Square, between 14th and 15th streets, features fine dining, sidewalk cafés, and live music.

© RICHARD CUMMINS / PHOTOPHILE

MERRY CHRISTMAS

FROM THE HOMEMADE WARMTH OF A Christmas tree in Littleton to the ho-ho hues of the City & County Building, Denver lights up for the holidays.

THE VIEW FROM THE COLORADO STATE Capitol frames a jewel of a city. Since its completion in 1908, the gold-domed facility (OPPOSITE TOP) has been a pillar of Denver's government community. Underneath, a network of tunnels (OPPOSITE BOTTOM), originally designed for transporting coal, link the state's official buildings.

A T THE CENTER OF THE STATE CAPITOL'S Greek cross floor plan, a magnificent rotunda rises 150 feet. Constructed of 128 pilasters, 60 spotlights, and 16 stained-glass windows, the Corinthian masterpiece caps the gallery of presidents (CENTER), located on the capitol's third floor. Offering an excellent view of the building's exterior, nearby Veteran's Monument (OPPOSITE), dedicated in 1990, honors the men and women of the armed services.

DEDICATED BY

THE PEOPLE OF COLORADO

IN GRATITUDE AND RESPECT

FOR THE MEN AND WOMEN

WHO HAVE PROUDLY SERVED

AND SACRIFICED

IN OUR NATION'S

ARMED FORCES

VETERANS DAY 1990

OVERLOOKING THE 16TH STREET MALL, the D&F Tower's 19-foot-tall clocks (TOP AND BOTTOM LEFT) might be considered Denver's most visible—although they certainly aren't alone in their quest to mark the passage of time.

ENVER'S OLDER COMMERCIAL AND residential buildings don't lose any of their architectural appeal, even in the shadows of the city's modern skyscrapers. The Church of the Holy Ghost (OPPOSITE), established in 1905, holds ground against the backdrop of the office tower at 1999 Broadway, the city's most recently built high-rise.

ALTHOUGH IT'S NOT THE LEAST BIT scandalous, nestled in the heart of downtown Denver is a true love triangle: the historic Brown Palace Hotel (LEFT). A favorite of presidents, celebrities, and travelers since 1892, the triangular building encompasses a nine-floor atrium lobby (OPPOSITE BOTTOM), where afternoon tea has become a tradition. The home of another Brown with a local claim to fame, the Molly Brown House Museum (OPPOSITE TOP) draws some 40,000 visitors annually. Once home to the Unsinkable Molly Brown—immortalized on stage and screen— the site opened in 1970 for tours that shed light on the lifestyle of Victorian Denver's upper crust.

THE OLD PROSPECTOR
In 1891, this 12' high, 400 lb. hand-
made copper statue was erected on the top
of the seven story Colorado Gold Mining
Stock Exchange building, on this site until
1962. The sculptor, Alphonse Pelzer,
modeled the statue after flamboyant and
colorful "Colonel" John William Straughan,
a civil war veteran, prospector and
wheelwright who lived from 1842-1903.

The statue symbolizes industry, patience
and enterprise.

WHILE THERE HAVE BEEN MANY golden moments in Denver's history, few compare to the thrills of a Nuggets basketball game. Since 1976, the Denver Nuggets have taken to the hardwood—of late, playing in the Pepsi Center, opened in 1999. More than 100 years earlier, a different kind of nugget ruled. To commemorate Denver's days as a mining capital, *The Old Prospector* stands outside the Brooks Towers downtown.

JUST NORTHWEST OF DENVER, CLEAR Creek History Park in Golden shows visitors the ways of life in the latter half of the 19th century. The living history site includes original 1800s log cabins, a one-room schoolhouse, and barns, and features re-creations of a blacksmith shop, root cellar, corral, smokehouse, and heirloom garden.

ONE OF THE REGION'S MOST cherished landmarks, Tiny Town (THIS PAGE) opened in 1915, just southeast of Denver. A miniature train and steam-powered locomotive encircle more than 100 one-sixth-scale buildings, many recently renovated for preservation. Full-scale restoration takes place in the city's historic residential neighborhoods, such as beautiful Curtis Park (OPPOSITE TOP), where diverse architectural styles hold sway. But more than its attractions and buildings, it is the people who have transformed Denver from a rugged mining outpost to a metropolitan center. The Black American West Museum & Heritage Center, under the leadership of founder Paul Stewart (OPPOSITE BOTTOM), celebrates the regional contributions of African-American cowboys.

RISING FROM THE EDGES OF THE CITY, the Foothills of the snow-capped Rocky Mountains transport travelers above the roar of the crowds toward a plethora of weekend getaway sites.

DON'T TRY THIS AT HOME. WELL, unless you happen to live in the Denver area, where aspen glens and icy cascades offer picturesque views.

NO MATTER WHAT THE SEASON, THE Rockies come alive for adventuresome hikers of all kinds. Michael Richardson (TOP) became the first African-American to climb all of Colorado's 54 "fourteeners"—peaks of at least 14,000-foot elevations. For more than 25 years, Gudy Gaskill (OPPOSITE) has been developing her reputation as a true trailblazer, soliciting and guiding volunteers to help build the Colorado Trail. Divided into 30 segments, the trail requires between six and eight weeks to walk in its entirety.

THINK SKIING, THINK VAIL. Between mid-October and mid-May, the slopes of Colorado's well-known resort town see around 300 inches of snow.

T O WAX PASTORALLY OF COLORADO'S scenic beauty simply doesn't do it justice. The region's crisp, cool waters provide a perfect spot for contemplation or for engaging in a favorite pastime.

D E N V E R

WEST OF LOWER DOWNTOWN, Cherry Creek and the South Platte River converge at Confluence Park, a prime urban recreation area. Local kayakers love the spot for its after-work convenience.

WITH SO MUCH TO DRAW FROM for inspiration, Denver artists maintain a full palette. Local painters William Matthews (TOP LEFT) and Quang Ho (TOP RIGHT) both have met with significant success in their field.

2165

KIDDIN' AROUND IN DENVER IS MADE all the more enjoyable by the area's wealth of sights and sounds. In the shadows of an aspen forest or in the heart of the city, bountiful fun awaits (PAGES 72-75).

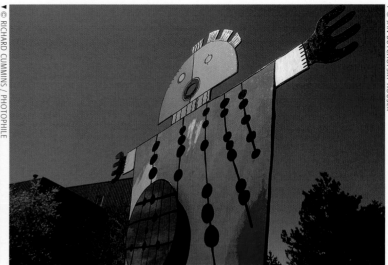

© CATHERINE GEHM

I T TAKES TWO TO ZOO, ALTHOUGH FOR some weary travelers, the excursion's a wee bit overwhelming. Understandably so: Nearly 4,000 animals call the Denver Zoo home.

THE COLORS OF DENVER'S FAUNA AND flora come alive in the city's parks and gardens. The 21-acre Denver Botanic Gardens (OPPOSITE TOP) is recognized as an authority on Rocky Mountain horticulture and features a Japanese Shofuen garden.

WHAT BEGAN AS A SEED OF AN IDEA in 1985 has turned into one of the country's most successful community programs. Denver Urban Gardens (TOP AND OPPOSITE) helps low-income inner-city families add fresh, healthy foods to their menus through some 60 gardens in the region. In the fields outside the city, migrant workers continue to play a role in tending to the land.

ROM THE LAND AND FROM THE WATERS, creatures great and small can be seen in Denver. Ocean Journey (THIS PAGE), the city's stunning $93 million aquarium, features hours of interactive fun on its 17-acre site. For a *Prehistoric Journey* (opposite), visit the Denver Museum of Nature and Science, with its Phipps IMAX Theater, gems and minerals, and 95 dioramas.

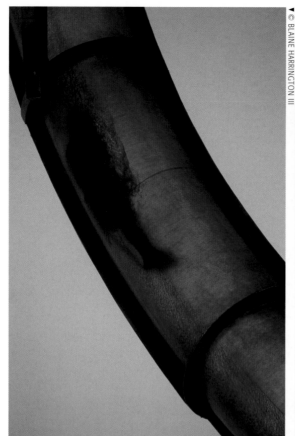

HRILLS AND EXCITEMENT AWAIT FUN lovers at Denver's Six Flags Elitch Gardens. The park's 49 major rides include Twister II, which reaches 100 feet at its peak.

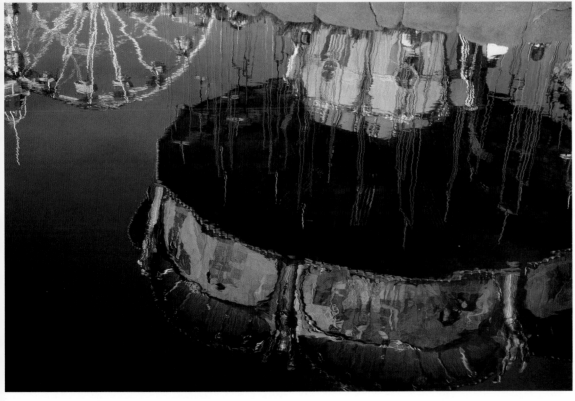

DESPITE A WELL-FOUNDED REPUTATION for getting blanketed with snow each year, Colorado also sees its share of rarer weather events: a brilliant rainbow over Littleton, or a twister dancing around in the distance.

NO OTHER GOLF IS ON PAR WITH ROCKY Mountain golf. Often nestled in the shadows of buttes and mountains, the area's greens invite even novice hackers to feel on top of their game.

THAT PRECIPITOUS MOUNTAINSIDE GOT your goat? Well, hang in there—tightly. Outdoor enthusiasts flock to the Denver area for its recreational amenities, which include plenty of rock climbing and bouldering locations.

REMOTE AREAS OF WILDERNESS ABOUND in Colorado, attracting every species, from the gentle lamb to the noble ram. The state Division of Wildlife works diligently with other outdoor and environmental groups to protect and restore the region's threatened and endangered species.

BUFFALO ONCE ROAMED FREELY IN the American West and continue to make a presence today as sources of folklore for the area. Equally memorialized, one of the area's frontiersmen is commemorated in statue in Golden. His prowess as a hunter on the western frontier earned William F. Cody the now-familiar nickname of Buffalo Bill (OPPOSITE, TOP LEFT).

DENVER

THE DENVER REGION HAS GROWN MORE and more popular over the years, but it continues to remain under the watchful gaze of those creatures who once claimed the land for their very own.

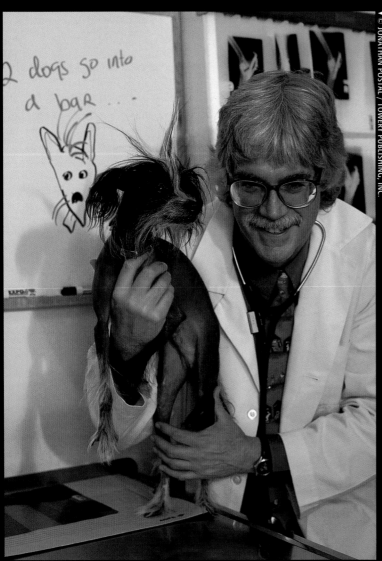

A COMMUNITY EFFORT SAVED DENVER's 1930 Mayan Theater (LEFT) from the wrecking ball in 1985, and art film lovers have reaped the benefits ever since. A facelift for the old Bluebird Theater (OPPOSITE), a former adult movie house, turned it into one of the city's hottest music venues. And, speaking of hot, have you heard the one about the veterinarian known for his sideline occupation as stand-up comedian and for his starring role on cable television's *Emergency Vets*? In fact, Dr. Kevin Fitzgerald (OPPOSITE, BOTTOM LEFT) is so popular that adoring female fans have set up a Web site in his honor. Evan Nelson (OPPOSITE, BOTTOM RIGHT), aka DJ Skunk, draws loyal followers of his own to the Snake Pit, a local music club where he opens up his Skunk Motel and spins nights of tunes and dancing.

BEAUTIFUL PEOPLE
450 720 950
HONG KONG ACTION!

GHOST DOG
430   930
MR. YUN-FAT "PRISON ON FIRE"

REAR WINDOW-4
CUP-715
FRIDAY &
SATURDAY M

ATTENDEES ARE BOUND TO HAVE FUN at any one of Denver's festivals and outdoor celebrations. Labor Day revelers celebrate the holiday at A Taste of Colorado (TOP), a food fest with music and children's activities on the side. Begun in 1971, the annual People's Fair (OPPOSITE TOP) raises funds for the Capitol Hill neighborhood.

© BLAINE HARRINGTON III

IT'S NOT A STRETCH TO SAY THE Colorado Ballet, founded in 1851, is art in the making. Under the leadership of Artistic Director and CEO Martin Fredmann (OPPOSITE LEFT), the organization is composed of 30 professional dancers.

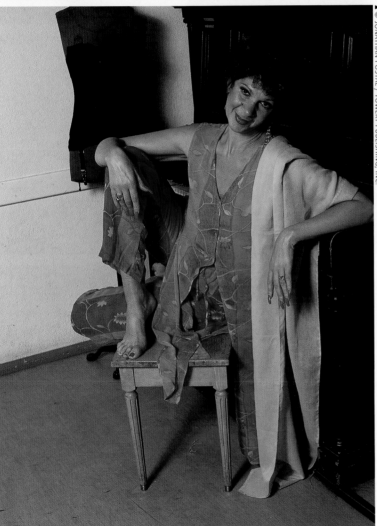

AFRICAN-AMERICAN ARTISTS MAKE A major contribution to Denver's arts scene, and each year, their efforts are celebrated at the Black Arts Festival (TOP). In 1970, Cleo Parker Robinson (BOTTOM LEFT)—a board member of the National Council on the Arts—founded a grassroots, multicultural modern dance troupe that has been thrilling audiences worldwide ever since. Cleo Parker Robinson Dance also includes a year-round school, 300-seat theater, and an outreach program for disadvantaged youth. Musician Otis Taylor (BOTTOM RIGHT) began his career in the 1960s, but quit the music business until 1995. His bluesy sound has experienced a resurgence of late, with new recordings and a growing following in the United States and Canada.

ALL THE WORLD'S A STAGE, AND WHATever your talent, Denver's got a snazzy place to showcase it. The 675,000-square-foot Pepsi Center (TOP)—home to the NBA's Denver Nuggets and the NHL's Colorado Avalanche—seats around 19,000 spectators for its events. Downtown's Denver Performing Arts Complex (OPPOSITE TOP) covers four city blocks and includes eight theaters and a ballroom. Touring Broadway plays and award-winning regional theatre and dance are just some of the entertainment to utilize the complex's facilities.

PERFORMANCES OF SUCH CLASSICS AS *Porgy and Bess* (THIS PAGE) invigorate the lineup of Opera Colorado. Capturing emotion on celluloid, Boulder resident and world-renowned avant-garde filmmaker Stan Brakhage (OPPOSITE) has influenced scores of directors from John Cassavetes to Martin Scorsese.

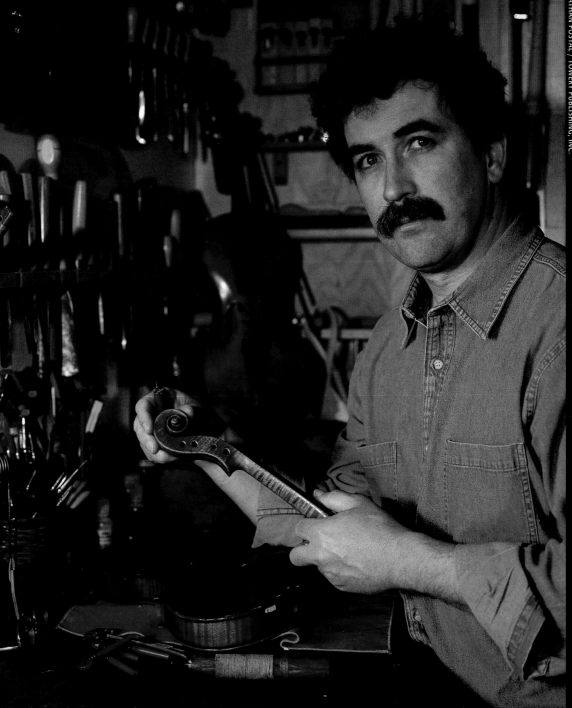

THERE ACTUALLY ARE SOME STRINGS attached when it comes to members of Denver's orchestral community. Basil Vendryes (LEFT) joined the Colorado Symphony Orchestra in 1993 and serves as its principal violist. Handcrafting and restoring violins, cellos, and violas, Von Bailey (OPPOSITE) operates from his shop on Denver's South Pearl Street.

© Richard Cummins / Photophile

© Charles Ledford / Stretch Photography

D ENVER'S NIGHTLIFE LIGHTS UP DOWN-town, particularly along the 16th Street Mall—the city's mile-long shopping and dining corridor. Home to Marlowe's and the Hard Rock Cafe, among others, the mall stretches from Market to Broadway.

Marlowe's

WHEN IT COMES TO RETRO, DENVER'S RIGHT IN line with other urban centers. In clubs around the city, martinis, swing dancing, and jive all have witnessed a resurgence.

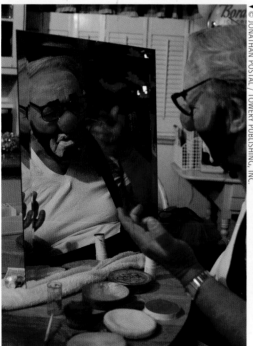

Once a Blinky the Clown, always a Blinky the Clown. Russell Scott became a Denver icon during his long tenure on television as the star of one of the city's most popular children's programs. These days, Scott spends much of his time at his collectibles store on South Broadway, but his makeup kit and big red nose are never far away.

ONE MAN'S TRASH IS ANOTHER MAN'S treasure—and for some Denverites, that makes for a pretty good living. Neptune's, under the ownership of Deni Buss (BOTTOM LEFT), is among the city's top vintage clothing stores. But it's old vinyl that Paul Epstein (BOTTOM RIGHT) has made a specialty at his shop, Twist and Shout, where a wide range of CDs, records, and tapes covers the sounds of today and yesterday.

6 am to 11 pm

PETE'S
KITCHEN

PARKING →

A TASTE OF THE TOWN THAT IS DENVER could mean anything from quaint diner breakfasts to quick donuts to café feasts prepared in the kitchen of Potager, a Capitol Hill restaurant owned by chef Teri Basoli (BOTTOM LEFT). Another Capitol Hill hot spot, Pete's Kitchen (OPPO-SITE) has become a late-night mainstay.

NO DRUGS OR NUCLEAR WEAPONS ALLOWED INSIDE

RESCUE THE RAINFOREST

UNIQUE SETTINGS ACCOMPANY THE menu items at some of Denver's better-known eateries. Rainforest Café (BOTTOM) surrounds diners with cascading waterfalls, live birds, and aquariums. But if simulated tropics aren't quite your style, check out the culinary combinations of executive chef Jeffrey French (OPPOSITE) at the Broker Restaurant on 17th Street. Patrons frequenting the money-themed establishment—housed in a former bank—will find themselves dining in a vault.

EVER ON THE MOVE, COLORADO'S perpetual motion encompasses heaven and earth. Abundant energy resources have made the state seventh in the nation in the production of natural gas, 10th in crude oil, and 12th in coal.

IN AUGUST 1993, POPE JOHN PAUL II LED
an estimated 375,000 worshippers in
mass for the seventh World Youth
Day celebration. The biennial event takes
place in a different international city
each time.

FOUNDED IN 1936, OUR LADY OF Guadalupe Church—under the guidance of Rev. Felix Lopez (OPPOSITE)—is among more than 40 Catholic congregations in Denver. Composed largely of Hispanic parishoners, the church has a long history of community activism.

BETH · HAMEDROSH · HAGODOL

Future Home of the Irish Community Center

ENVERITES CELEBRATE A MODERN mixture of beliefs and traditions. Active in numerous social and political causes, Rabbi Steven Foster (OPPO-SITE) leads congregants at Temple Emanuel. The former Beth Hamedrosh Hagodol Syna-gogue in the City Park West neighborhood has been many things over its 81 years—including a rave site called Sin-a-Go-Go. But in the hands of the local Irish community, a $7 million restoration will result in yet another life for the three-story structure.

IF THOU DESIRE REST DESIRE NOT TOO MUCH

I N DENVER, REST FOR THE WEARY OFTEN
manifests itself in monumental ways.
While the inner city offers streetwise
respite, its outskirts harbor quiet repose
(PAGES 132-135).

FEDERAL, STATE, AND LOCAL GOVERN-
mental offices rule in the Denver
area, home to various courts and a
division of the U.S. Mint. Making change of
a different sort, Colorado Supreme Court
Judge Mary J. Mullarkey (OPPOSITE) became
the state's first female chief justice in 1998.

LOCALS LOVE THEIR PUBLIC SERVANTS SO much, they've devoted a museum to some of them. Old Fire House No. 1, built in 1909, now houses the Denver Firefighters Museum (OPPOSITE TOP). Artifacts, old photos, and early fire-fighting vehicles are among the items on display at the downtown attraction.

© JONATHAN POTTER / POTTER PUBLISHING, INC.

ESTIGES OF DENVER'S FRONTIER-outpost past prevail today in signage, statues, and monuments around the region (PAGES 140-143). And in certain ways, history repeats itself: Members of the police department's mounted horse patrol unit (OPPOSITE) prefer to ride the equine express when keeping downtown streets safe.

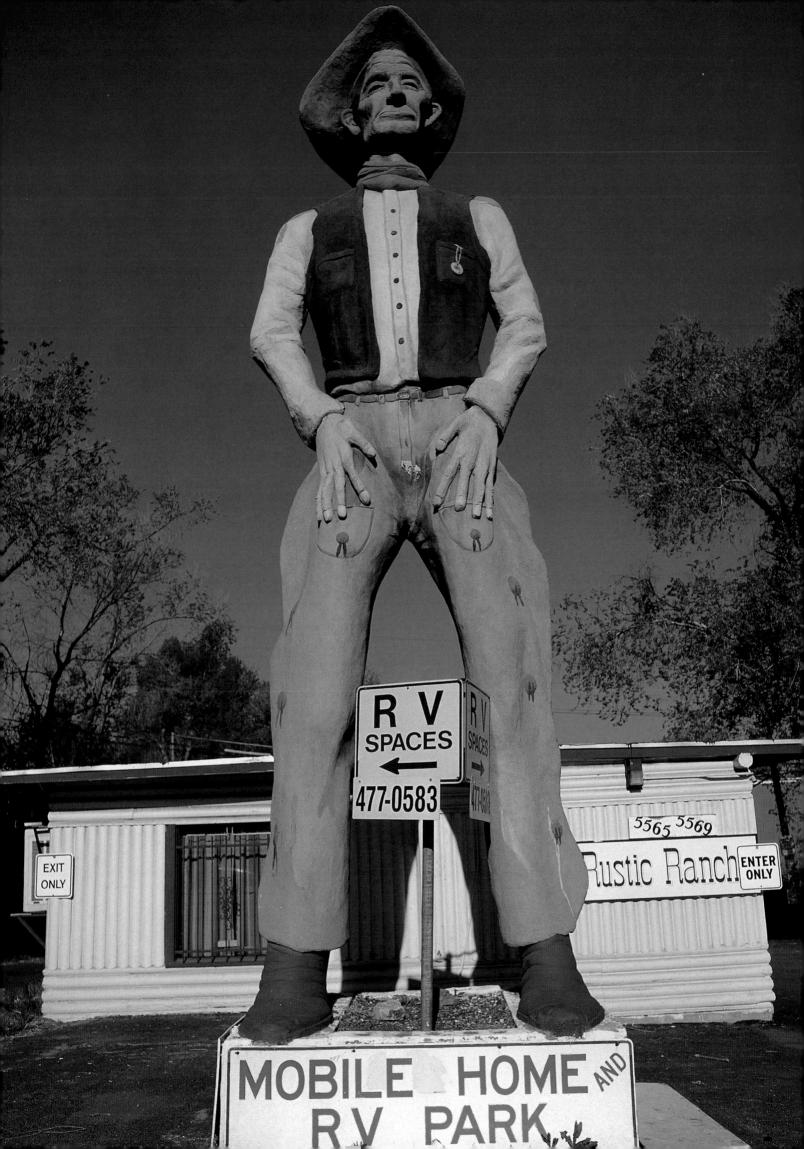

R IDING AND ROPING TRADITIONS STILL thrive on the thousands of acres of ranchland that encircle Denver. On modern cattle farms and weekend dude ranches, and in celebrations around the state, the ways of the Old West are revered.

TRADITIONS DIE HARD IN THE NEW OLD West. Luthier Edward V. Dick (BOTTOM) blends wood and sound into fine, handcrafted string instruments— including one of his own invention, the banjola, a combination of the banjo and mandolin. When locals aren't strummin' on the ol' banjola, they can turn to Rockmount Ranch Wear for classic western clothing. Operated in the LoDo district since 1946, the manufacturing and retail company is run by the Weil family (OPPOSITE TOP, FROM LEFT)—Jack Sr., grandson Steve, greatgrandson Colter, and Jack Jr.

HILE MANY IN DENVER STILL KNOW which end of the cow gets up first, the city long ago shed its image as a western outpost. Contemporary images of frontier themes continue to appear—albeit in some whimsical fashions.

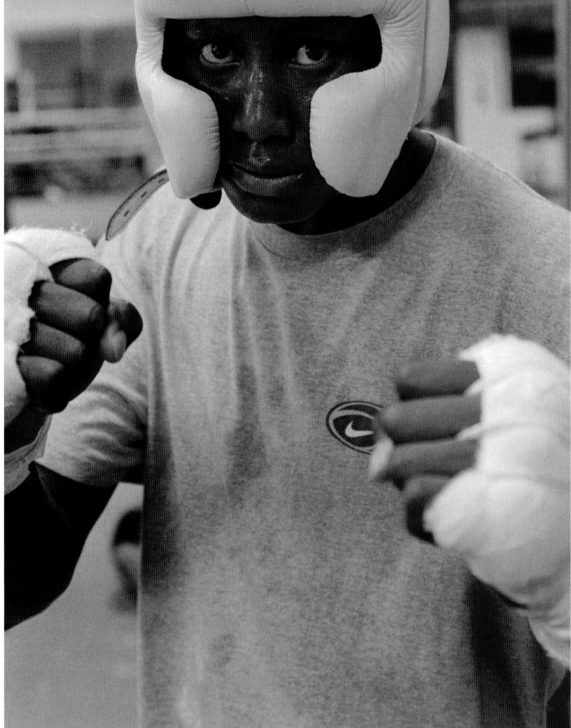

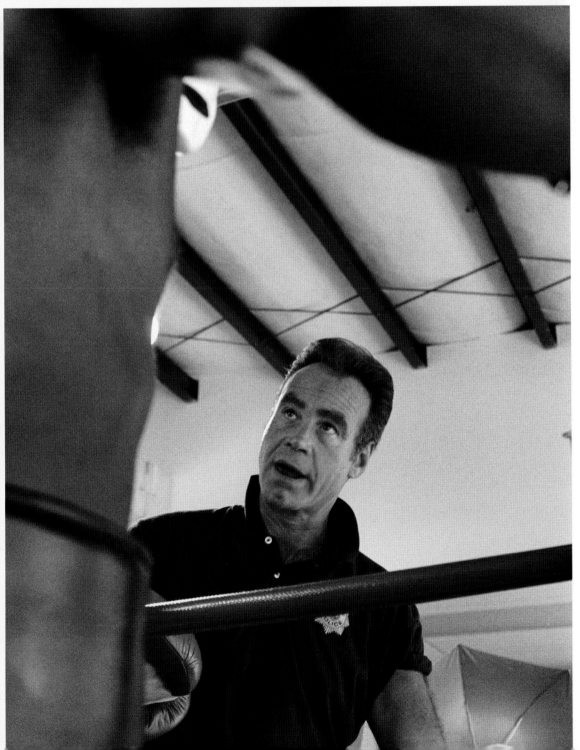

SOME THINGS IN LIFE ARE WORTH puttin' up your dukes and fighting for. Trainer Larry Goossen (BOTTOM) shows boxers the ropes in the gym of Denver-based promoter America Presents. In the political arena, thousands challenged the iron-fisted rule of the East Berlin government in 1989, and successfully brought down the Berlin Wall. A commemorative sculpture, *The Day the Wall Came Down* (OPPOSITE TOP), was once on display in Denver–hometown to its creator, sculptor Veryl Goodnight. In 1998, the piece was given to the people of Germany.

THE DENVER AREA'S MEDICAL FACILITIES rival those of any other metropolitan region. In addition to its state-of-the-art neonatal unit, Englewood's Swedish Medical Center (OPPOSITE) provides a full spectrum of health care coverage. Dr. Alden Harken (RIGHT) heads up the University of Colorado Health Sciences Center as professor and chairman of the Department of Surgery. Located in the heart of the city, the teaching and research facility is the only academic health center in the state.

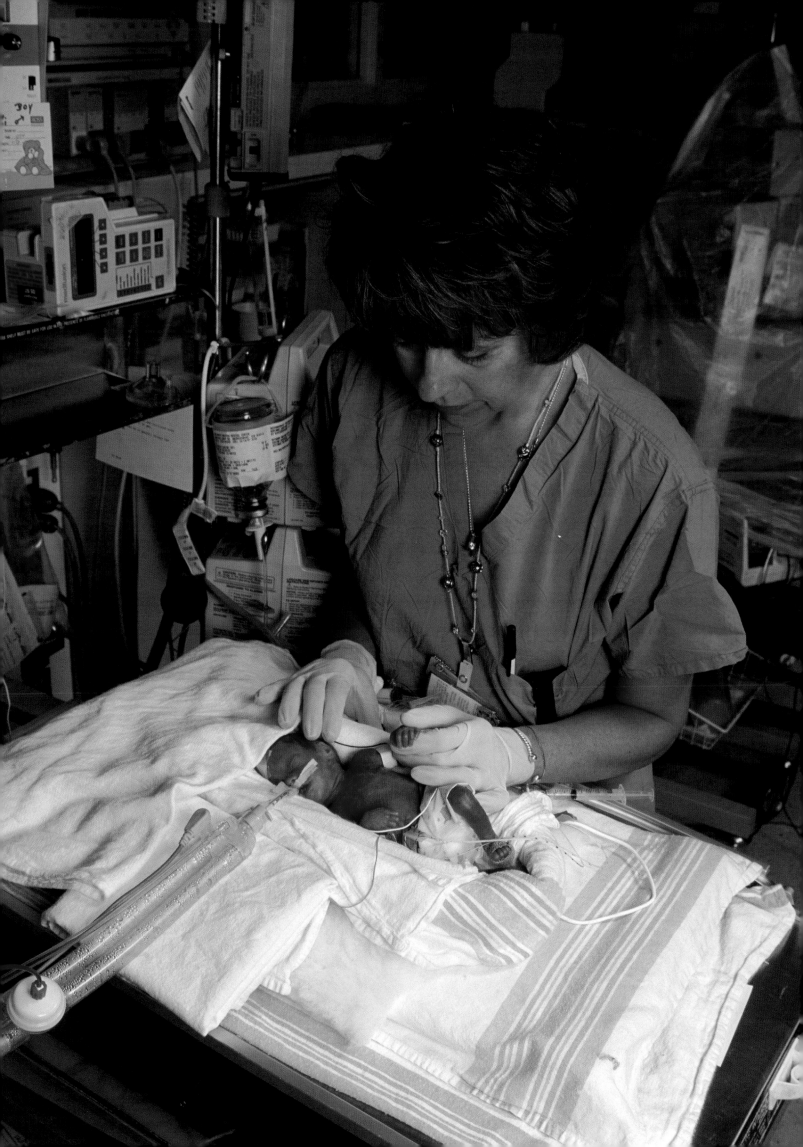

ARE ALL PUT ON THIS EARTH TO LEAVE IT A BETTE
FOR OUR HAVING BEEN HERE . . ."

A MULTITUDE OF VOICES CONTRIBUTES to the Denver community. Speaking out for the region's Hispanic sector, the award-winning newspaper *La Voz*, under editor and publisher Wanda Padilla (BOTTOM), celebrated its 25th anniversary in 2000. A bronze bust by Tsuyako Kaneko commemorates the contributions of Minoru Yasui, former World War II Japanese-American detainee and director of Denver's Commission on Community Relations.

AT WORK OR AT PLAY, LOCALS FIND THE infectious spirit of Denver uplifting— whether the activity is organized or improvised (PAGES 156-159).

AVING A BALL IN THE MILE HIGH CITY turned into jubilant celebration in 1998, when the Denver Broncos brought home the Vince Lombardi Trophy after winning Super Bowl XXXII. The coveted sports victory became just one more reason for the city to find itself sitting on top of the world.

Denver: Profiles in Excellence

A look at the corporations, businesses, professional groups, and community service organizations that have made this book possible. Their stories—offering an informal chronicle of the local business community—are arranged according to the date they were established in the Denver area.

Alpine Lumber Company ● Aspen Petroleum Products ● Aurora Public Schools ● CIBER Inc. ● Clear Channel Colorado ● Colorado Heart Imaging ● Colorado Office of Economic Development and International Trade ● Community Colleges of Colorado ● Denver Broncos Football Club ● Denver Business Journal ● Denver Rocky Mountain News ● Durrant ● Foster and Son ● Freeman Group Public Relations ● The Gates Rubber Company ● HenryGill Advertising ● Insurance Design & Placement, Inc. ● KeyBank/McDonald Investments Inc. ● Kimsey Electrical Contracting ● Kodak Colorado ● Level 3 Communications, Inc. ● Lucent Technologies NetworkCare Knowledge Center ● Marriott ● McGuckin Hardware ● Merrill Lynch & Company ● Pacific Western Technologies, Ltd. ● PEAK Resources Inc. ● People's Choice Transportation ● The Phil Long Dealerships

1859-1960

1859	Denver Rocky Mountain News
1885	Aurora Public Schools
1911	The Gates Rubber Company
1921	Merrill Lynch & Company
1930	PorterCare Adventist Health
1930	Rocky Mountain Orthodontics
1945	The Phil Long Dealerships
1948	Denver Business Journal
1955	McGuckin Hardware
1959	Foster and Son
1960	Denver Broncos Football Club

From knapsacks to backpacks and blackboards to keyboards, the Aurora Public School System (APS) has kept pace with the changing needs of society for more than 115 years. Today, APS is a thriving entity, comprising 44 schools that address the academic needs of more than 29,000 students—but there were humble beginnings. ● Traveling on horseback, William Smith set out on the campaign trail in 1885, visiting his neighbors along the Highline Canal and gathering signatures to organize School District 28. Smith's commitment to education was further evidenced by his donation of the land on which the

first one-room school was erected, and by his 50-year term on the Aurora School Board, the longest term ever served by an APS board member. Still in use, Aurora's first high school was dedicated in 1931 and named in Smith's honor.

Bill Hinkley, whose name became synonymous in APS with growth and forward movement, served as school superintendent from 1949 to 1968. Bill Murray, retired director of media services and resident historian, speaks fondly of Hinkley: "He was a strong influence in bringing the city and the school district together. Back in 1949, when Hinkley came on board, there was no money for supplies. He found surplus green standard military paper for us to use. It measured 8 inches by 10 inches, with two holes in the top. I also got two red pencils a year with which to grade papers. I imagine some of that green paper is still around."

Community Ties

APS has long played a role in helping the city of Aurora become a vibrant metropolitan community, according to Debbie Lynch, APS' director of communications. "Schools are the thread that ties the community together," Lynch says.

"The school district pulls people together."

An urban school district, APS finds 72 languages spoken among members of its student body. Educating the children of this community is serious business for APS. With its focus on excellence, APS is recognized nationally as a leader in curriculum development and performance standards.

An Educated Workforce

With Denver International Airport to the east, and Buckley Air Force Base, the University of Colorado Health Sciences Center, and the redeveloped Lowry Air Force Base—now a burgeoning business park and residential area—as neighbors,

Aurora's local industry calls for an educated workforce. APS answers that call.

"It is absolutely critical in our world of technology for students to be up to speed," says Lynch. "We're ensuring that they are." The passage of a $70 million bond issue in 1995 has enabled APS to renovate schools and update classrooms. In addition, some $20 million was earmarked for computers and related technology.

Now, skilled APS graduates need look no farther than their doorsteps for career choices. In keeping with the school district's mission statement, APS is dedicated to "developing lifelong learners who contribute to their community and succeed in a changing world."

Clockwise from top:
Fletcher Elementary School, Aurora Public School's (APS) newest elementary school, represents growth in north Aurora.

The Old William Smith High School was built in 1931.

APS is educating the workforce of the future.

APS places high value on the arts.

Denver Rocky Mountain News

When 28-year-old William Byers hauled a press into town on a wagon in 1859, Denver was a community of rowdy gold camps, a true frontier town. He set up shop on the top floor of Dick Wooton's log store, choosing the location because it had sturdy plank floors and the only glass windows in town. Working furiously to beat "Jolly" Jack Merrick for the honor of publishing Denver's first newspaper, Byers published his debut issue of the *Denver Rocky Mountain News* on April 23. Merrick folded his *Cherry Creek Pioneer* after one issue and headed for the hills in search of gold. This contest set a tone of journalistic competitiveness that lasted almost 150 years.

Denver's status as a one-newspaper town did not last long. Thomas Gibson, Byers' former business partner, launched the city's first daily newspaper, the *Herald*, on May 1, 1860. Four years later, he sold the paper, and its name was changed to the *Daily Commonwealth and Republican*. That same year, the *News* was nearly wiped out by a flash flood, and Byers' home was lost to the swelling waters of Cherry Creek. Territorial Governor John Evans, a silent partner in the *Commonwealth*, gave the Byers family shelter and opened his newspaper columns to the young newspaperman. Six weeks later, Byers and his business partner, John L. Dailey, bought out the *Commonwealth* for $4,000, putting the *News* back on the streets.

Shortly after the end of the Civil War, the *Denver Daily Gazette* began publication, the product of Frederick J. Stanton, a staunch Democrat and nemesis of Byers, a loyal Republican. The fierce rivalry even took to the streets in 1869 when Stanton hit Byers on the head with a cane. While Byers survived, Stanton's paper did not; the *Gazette* went under in May 1869.

A Formidable Opponent

During the late 1800s, Denver's population grew to more than 100,000 residents, all of whom were hungry for news. Responding to the city's steady growth, the *News'* most formidable opponent, the *Denver Post*, first appeared as a weekly in 1892.

During this time, the *News'* ownership shifted several times before Scripps Howard newspapers purchased it in 1926. Scripps Howard combined the *News* with the struggling *Denver Express,* creating the *Denver Evening News*, to supplement the morning *News*.

The *Post-News* rivalry swelled: The *News* dispatched paperboys out onto the streets to give away papers, and both publications sponsored extravagant contests. They even offered free gasoline during the great gasoline war of February 1927. In April 1942, in order to differentiate itself from its competitor, the *News* switched to its now-trademark tabloid format.

A State-of-the-Art Publication

Today, the *News'* operations are a far cry from the dim composing rooms where ink literally hung in the air. Gone are the days of molten-lead typesetting and clacking machinery adjacent to the newsroom. Today, the *News* is Colorado's largest newspaper, with a Sunday circulation of some 552,000 and a daily circulation of about 446,000.

At the modern E.W. Estlow production facility, a 400,000-square-foot plant that opened in 1992, five Goss Colorliner presses print nearly 70,000 newspapers per hour on each press. Unmanned vehicles, guided

The *Denver Rocky Mountain News* was founded in 1859 by William Byers on the top floor of Dick Wooton's log store (top). Today the paper is located in the heart of downtown Denver (bottom).

Cited repeatedly for editorial excellence, the paper has collected far more first-place editorial awards from the AP of Colorado and the Colorado Press Association than its competitors. The *News* was named Colorado's best metro daily newspaper five years running by the Associated Press. Recently, it earned one of journalism's highest prizes, the 2000 Pulitzer Prize for breaking news photography, for its coverage of the April 1999 tragedy at Columbine High School. The Pulitzer board honored the photo staff for its "powerful collection of emotional images taken after the student shootings at Columbine High School."

In addition, the *News* leads the nation in advertising inches, ranking first in total full-run inches and tops in color advertising. In 1999, the paper ran 7.2 million classified ads, which earned it another top ranking nationwide.

The *Denver Rocky Mountain News* is delivered to the doorsteps of more than 660,000 Denver-area readers every day.

by copper wiring in the concrete floor, wheel one-ton rolls of newsprint in one of the most modern printing plants in the world.

In addition, a newsroom team of approximately 200 people operates on a multimillion-dollar budget to bring the news to metro Denver readers. Reporters compose stories from the scene on laptop computers and call in breaking news on cell phones. Photographers use digital cameras and download images from their cameras into computers. Photos, graphic art, headlines, and type are all assembled on Macintosh computers in the newsroom at the *News'* headquarters on West Colfax Avenue.

And at the *News'* Web site—www.rockymountainnews.com—readers can access the paper's top stories, get Associated Press (AP) updates on breaking news, and search the *News'* archives of stories dating back to 1989.

Awards and Contributions

Like its predecessors, today's *News* remains active in the community. The company is part owner of the Colorado Rockies National League baseball club, and sponsors many public events, including the Cherry Creek Arts Festival. In 1999 alone, the *News* returned $4.8 million to 130 local charities.

A Strategic Truce

On May 11, 2000, the *Denver Rocky Mountain News* and the *Denver Post* declared a truce in the nation's last great newspaper war. The two dailies agreed to merge their business operations, but maintain separate newsrooms in what is known as a joint operating agreement.

"The journalism war of the last 140 years has exacted a cost that threatens this community's rich newspaper heritage," says Kenneth Lowe, president and chief operating officer of the E.W. Scripps Co., which owns the *News*. "It has been a long, historic battle."

At the modern E.W. Estlow production facility, a 400,000-square-foot plant that opened in 1992, five Goss Colorliner presses print nearly 70,000 newspapers per hour on each press.

The Gates Rubber Company has kept millions of cars—whether the Model Ts of the 1910s or the SUVs of the 21st century—cruising the world's highways for almost 100 years. The company has evolved from a small, suburban manufacturer to the largest non-tire-producing rubber company in the world, employing generations of Coloradans at the company's historic Denver plant. ● But the outlook for The Gates Rubber Company was not always so auspicious. Charles Gates purchased the Colorado Tire and Leather Company in the fall of 1911, sinking his life savings into a tire shop that he thought was a

success, but turned out not to meet his expectations. The business' viability had been misrepresented—the bills clearly outweighed the orders.

Gates, however, rose to the challenge. Initially, the company's only product was the leather Durable Tread. Motorists fastened these steel-studded bands to their flimsy car tires to extend their mileage. The company had a solid product, but a limited market: The number of cars in Denver at that time did not exceed 5,000. Gates and his brother John Gates worked diligently to develop persuasive advertising and promotions that would appeal to the larger East Coast market, and within eight months, the business was turning a profit.

Leather to Rubber

The emergence of a new material helped transform the Colorado Tire and Leather Company to the International Rubber Company. Rubber was flexible, temperature-resilient, and ideal for making tires, hoses, belts, and many other products. Using this remarkable product, Gates was able to improve his famous retreads, and the Half-Sole soon replaced the Durable Tread.

Although the Half-Sole continued to bring profit to the company, its next product took the auto industry by storm. In 1917, John Gates invented the world's first rubber and fabric V-belt. Suddenly, leather was obsolete, as rubber proved more durable under the hoods of America's cars.

As the demand for the company's products grew, so too did the need for manufacturing space. Moving the company from downtown, Charles Gates went south to the suburbs. The South Broadway site remains a landmark in South Denver, and the Gates beacon, a water tower bearing an encircled logo, is still visible today to travelers on Interstate 25.

When the United States entered World War I, The Gates Rubber Company was there to aid in the war effort. Because it used less rubber than similar products, the Half-Sole was considered a priority product, which meant increased sales contracts for the company. At the conclusion of the war, rubber prices dropped and tires became less expensive to replace. The company phased out the Half-Sole and introduced a new product, the balloon tire.

At the onset of the 1920s, The Gates Rubber Company began to diversify. Along with the production of tires and V-belts, the company added molded rubber goods such as garden hoses, hydraulic seals, hog paddles, and, eventually, radiator hoses. During the Great Depression, the company prospered, engineering new products while staying loyal to employees and customers.

Progress Continues

Charles Gates' philosophy was simple—make things that people would always need. And in World War II, there was an obvious need for the products the company made. The problem, however, was the rubber supply. As Japan invaded the rubber-producing countries, the Allies lost 90 percent of their raw material supply.

In response to this crisis, The Gates Rubber Company joined other manufacturers to develop a synthetic rubber. As a result of this venture, on August 29, 1943, the company was awarded the Army/Navy E Award for excellence. The development of

synthetic rubber helped boost the company's productivity and profit further; from 1946 to 1954, sales revenues increased from $59 million to $82 million.

"We had to keep looking for new apples to polish," says Charles Gates Jr., executive vice president, noting that, in 1954, Gates went multinational—setting up shop first in Canada and then in Mexico. Shortly thereafter, The Gates Rubber Company established plants in Illinois, Iowa, North Carolina, and Tennessee.

New Challenges

The 1990s brought the biggest changes for the company. The Denver facility stopped manufacturing belts and became the primary location for administrative and corporate offices. The Gates Energy Products division, the industrial battery business, and the Gates Molded Products Company were sold as well.

The most profound change occurred in 1996 when Gates became a wholly owned subsidiary of Tomkins PLC, a diversified

Charles Gates is the founder of The Gates Rubber Company.

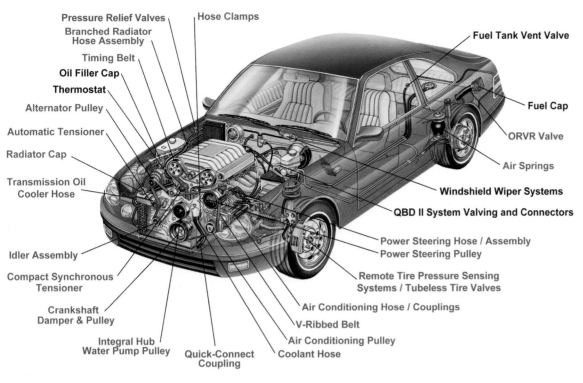

Pressure Relief Valves
Branched Radiator Hose Assembly
Timing Belt
Oil Filler Cap
Thermostat
Alternator Pulley
Automatic Tensioner
Radiator Cap
Transmission Oil Cooler Hose
Idler Assembly
Compact Synchronous Tensioner
Crankshaft Damper & Pulley
Integral Hub Water Pump Pulley
Quick-Connect Coupling
Coolant Hose
Air Conditioning Pulley
V-Ribbed Belt
Air Conditioning Hose / Couplings
Remote Tire Pressure Sensing Systems / Tubeless Tire Valves
Power Steering Pulley
Power Steering Hose / Assembly
QBD II System Valving and Connectors
Windshield Wiper Systems
Air Springs
ORVR Valve
Fuel Cap
Fuel Tank Vent Valve
Hose Clamps

■ GATES RUBBER COMPANY   ■ STANT COMPANIES   ■ SCHRADER BRIDGEPORT

industrial management company based in the United Kingdom. At the time, Gates was the largest non-tire-producing rubber company in the world. Its plants and its distribution and sales centers boasted a profit in annual sales of more than $1.6 billion.

Now referred to as The Gates Group of Companies, the firm employs approximately 24,000 people who operate more than 63 factories and 43 distribution centers in 18 countries. The focus of the organization can still be seen in its three major product groups:

Worldwide Power Transmission, Worldwide Hydraulic, and Industrial Hose & Connectors.

Since the acquisition by Tomkins, Gates has grown aggressively. The company acquired the Stant Companies, Trico Products, and Schrader-Bridgeport—companies known for manufacturing products for original automotive manufacturers and the replacement markets. Among these products are integrated windshield wiper systems and components, wiper blades and refills, thermostats, heater cores, hose clamps, power steering system products,

fluid control system components, lubrication equipment, greases and oils, and tire hardware and accessories.

In projections for its future, The Gates Rubber Company sees the business continuing in its role as a quality innovator and industry leader in the auto industry. Building relationships through sales and service, as well as integrating new and innovative companies into the Gates group, will ensure the ongoing success that has distinguished the company from its inception.

Since the acquisition by Tomkins, Gates has grown aggressively. The company acquired the Stant Companies, Trico Products, and Schrader-Bridgeport— companies known for manufacturing products for original automotive manufacturers and the replacement markets.

The Gates Rubber Company's South Broadway site is a landmark in South Denver.

Merrill Lynch & Company

With total client assets of more than $1.7 trillion, Merrill Lynch & Company is a leader in financial planning and financial management for individuals and small businesses. Among its offerings are trading and brokering, investment banking and advisory services, trading of foreign exchange, commodities and derivatives, banking and lending insurance, and research. Opening new offices across the state and offering increased services to a population awash in newfound prosperity, Merrill Lynch & Company is fostering a new kind of success for Colorado—the likes of which have not been seen since the gold rush of the 1850s or the oil boom in the 1970s.

Merrill Lynch & Company established its Cherry Creek office in April 2000.

Expansion and Opportunity

The Centennial State is now home to five of the nation's fastest-growing counties, ranks third in population growth, and has reestablished itself as Wall Street West, as financial interests such as Merrill Lynch—the largest securities firm in the United States—takes the lead.

"We have made a commitment to Colorado by opening six new offices here," says Guy Williams, first vice president and managing director of Merrill Lynch's Mountain District. The expansion comes atop Merrill Lynch's already significant presence in the Denver area when, in 1994, the New York securities firm marked Denver's economic turnaround by announcing a major expansion and construction of a new office campus in Douglas County, the fastest-growing county in America. Today, the Meridian Business Park is home to Merrill Lynch's service center, where some 2,500 people work on a 70-acre site nestled against the Rocky Mountains.

Williams previously headed Merrill Lynch offices in San Diego, but, in 1998, relocated to the Denver area when the district office was moved in response to Colorado's thriving economy. "Nothing that I saw in San Diego compares with the growth here," says Williams. "Our services here are very high end. For example, our trust department was a one-man band up until last summer. But with all the economic

growth in Colorado, now our trust department is a significant part of our operations."

Also significant is Merrill Lynch's strategic location of new offices in such upscale locales as Aspen and in Denver's Cherry Creek North, where the former offices of the Archdiocese of Denver were converted into Merrill Lynch Plaza. Eight institutional traders and 24 financial consultants, headed by Jodi Rolland, vice president and director, now work in the heart of the vibrant business district.

Merrill Lynch also followed the high-end growth to other parts of the state, opening new offices in Castle Rock, Lakewood, and Highlands Ranch. Additionally, the company relocated into new expansive offices in Colorado Springs, as well as in Boulder and Fort Collins.

Philanthropic Efforts

Merrill Lynch has established a tradition of philanthropic giving, including a generous scholarship and grant program that today remains a strong vestige of founder Charles E. Merrill. Merrill believed that prosperity grows by opening the marketplace to all and that education opens doors.

Since 1992, the company has had a mentoring partnership with Creighton Middle School and Molholm Elementary School in Lakewood to improve the achievements of at-risk students.

Merrill Lynch also enjoys a long tradition of being a premier place to work, with employee benefits touted as some of the best in the nation. In 1999, *Colorado Parent* magazine named Merrill Lynch one of the top companies in Colorado for working parents.

Merrill Lynch offers a variety of services, including trust services (left).

Jodi Rolland serves as director of Merrill Lynch's Cherry Creek office (right).

Fortune named Merrill Lynch one of the 100 best companies to work for in America, and *Latina Style* named it one of the 50 best companies for Hispanic women.

At the company's core are highly trained financial advisers who assist a range of clients, whether they are parents who want to grow a family business, yet secure the future for future generations, or a CEO who wants to take the initiative to transform a company.

"We look at the goals of our clients and create a program to help them achieve those goals," says Rolland, who not only helps people realize their financial dreams, but also has helped them find their financial past. A man named Joe, for example, was an elderly client Rolland worked with to put together a trust.

"He never made a lot of money, but he saved every penny that he made," says Rolland. "He kept bringing in his stock certificates. We got him to an attorney, spent four evenings going through all his boxes, and found he had

$3.5 million. Now, he's putting the next two generations through college. These are the kind of stories we encounter, and we feel so fortunate to be able to help people like Joe."

Founder Merrill—a small-town Florida doctor's son who found his true talent on Wall Street—would be proud that his legacy lives on. Early on, he believed that the opportunities of the markets should be accessible to everyone, which led to his life's work of "bringing Wall Street to Main Street."

The new offices at Cherry Creek were designed with high-net-worth clients in mind.

Englewood is home to Merrill Lynch's Mountain District offices (left).

Merrill Lynch's July 2000 ribbon-cutting ceremony was attended by Denver Mayor Wellington Webb (right).

PorterCare Adventist Health

PorterCare Adventist Health came about largely because of a check for 45 cents. In 1928, pioneer businessman Henry M. Porter was traveling in California when he fell ill. At Paradise Valley Sanitarium in National City, he received excellent care. On his return to Denver, a 45-cent check arrived in the mail. Enclosed was a letter from Paradise Valley Credit Manager Harley Rice, apologizing for an inadvertent overcharge. The impact on Porter was profound. ● That was not the first time Porter had been impressed with a hospital operated by the Seventh-day Adventists. Twenty-five years earlier, he had been a

patient at Glendale Sanitarium, also in California, and had taken note of both the quality of his care and the compassion of the staff. At one point, Porter offered a tip to a young therapist, who politely declined. "The first person I ever met who refused money," Porter would later say.

Porter became increasingly convinced that Denver should have a similar kind of hospital. He donated 40 acres on South Downing Street—at that time on the outskirts of the city. At first, leaders of the Adventist Church hesitated—concerned about shaky times and financial struggles at other sanitariums. But in 1929, construction crews began work. Porter's daughter, Dora Porter Mason, added a sizable donation toward the building.

On February 16, 1930, Porter Sanitarium and Hospital opened. Minutes from board meetings and written testimonials from that time describe a legacy of commitment and compassion that continues today. Just like their predecessors, today's staff members are dedicated to continuing the legacy of compassion, integrity, and quality that Porter himself experienced.

Whole-Person Care

The pioneers of Adventist health care put into practice an important philosophy: Don't just fix people up when they come to a hospital—do whatever possible to help them understand how to live well, so they won't have such a need for hospital care. Today, this practice is called preventive medicine; back then, it was a way of life, a realization that the care of the body should not be divorced from the care of the mind and the soul. It is a belief that when people live well—exercise, eat well, and get proper rest, recreation, and spiritual care—their whole being is healthier, minimizing the need for medical interventions such as surgery and medication.

The Adventists had a reputation for whole-person care provided at sanitariums. The most famous facility was Battle Creek Sanitarium in Michigan, where John Harvey Kellogg, the inventor of corn flakes, was medical director. Colorado was blessed with a similar institution in Boulder, established in 1896. In 1962, the Boulder facility became known as Boulder Memorial Hospital, and

in 1990, it relocated to Louisville and became Avista Adventist Hospital.

In 1963, Porter Sanitarium and Hospital took the name Porter Memorial Hospital. It is now called Porter Adventist Hospital. Both the Boulder and the Denver facilities have matured into full-fledged community hospitals, with emergency rooms, obstetrics units, ICUs, and outpatient care.

Henry M. Porter is the founder of what is today known as PorterCare Adventist Health.

Porter Adventist Hospital has a long history of quality care. Pictured here is the north wing.

Pictured here is the original Porter Memorial Hospital building.

A New Hospital in the South

In 1989, Porter Memorial Hospital opened Littleton Hospital on South Broadway, near rapidly growing Douglas County. Now called Littleton Adventist Hospital, this impressive facility is expanding to meet community needs. Porter, Littleton, and Avista Adventist hospitals today stand as testament to a therapist who long ago gave excellent care and refused a tip, to a young credit manager who took time to send a 45-cent refund, and to a businessman with a generous heart and visionary spirit.

The legacy of the hospital's founder is reflected in its mission today: "To provide renewed hope, health, and well-being for people in the community." The statement of vision makes the legacy specific: "To be a sanctuary of compassion, integrity, excellence, stewardship, and creativity; reflecting the healing ministry of Christ."

In 1996, Porter, Littleton, and Avista Adventist hospitals affiliated with Centura Health—a statewide, not-for-profit health care organization.

The Value of the Human Spirit

Despite the pressures of America's health care system in the new millennium, PorterCare Adventist Health, the hospitals' parent organization, remains committed to compassion, integrity, and high-quality service, with a keen interest in health rather than a focus limited to sickness and treatment.

The value of the human spirit is part of the picture. Nearly every day, a prayer is offered over the public address systems at each PorterCare Adventist Health hospital, and volunteer prayer teams receive requests and invite the power of God to work where there is particular need. While these practices remain a matter of faith, numerous scientific studies in recent years demonstrate the effectiveness of prayer in helping patients experience quicker recoveries and fewer complications. The spiritual aspect is not about a particular theology or belief system—it is simply about reaching out to the human spirit with the compassion demonstrated in the ministry of Jesus 2,000 years ago.

The Medical Office Building at Porter Adventist Hospital houses outpatient surgery departments.

Rocky Mountain Orthodontics

The Rocky Mountain Orthodontics (RMO) effort began around 1930. Since then, the company has made dramatic advances in the science of orthodontics, establishing itself as one of the leaders of a rapidly evolving field— a field that down through the decades has made people's lives better. Since its formal incorporation in 1935 as Rocky Mountain Metal Products, RMO has been known as a company of energy and ideas—traits that remain at the core of the company's philosophy today. ● RMO is much more than a $45 million business

and model of excellence among Colorado corporations. The company is the oldest privately held orthodontic firm in the United States, and is a Denver institution whose company history is inextricably linked with the history of Denver and orthodontics itself.

Innovation and Determination

Before the advent of chrome alloy (stainless steel) and prior to the founding of RMO, orthodontists had to be skilled craftsmen as well as doctors. In fact, much of their time was spent devising, constructing, and maintaining their own oral appliances. Because those appliances were typically fabricated from gold alloy, which tended to loosen in a short period of time, a large part of an orthodontist's work was dedicated to repairing and adjusting the appliances after they had been put into use.

The orthodontist's job demanded mechanical skill, diligence, and even artistry. And yet, for all of the effort involved, the occupation was often less than rewarding. Even the best orthodontic appliances of the day were woefully limited in their effectiveness.

All that changed with the development of versatile stainless steel alloys, coupled with the ingenuity and foresight of RMO's founder, Dr. Archie Brusse, a pioneer Denver orthodontist. With a small but capable staff, and with help from an executive at the American Steel and Wire Company, RMO set about developing the first set of prefabricated orthodontic appliance options. After much clinical research and experimentation, the first system of options was unveiled in 1933 at the annual meeting of the American Association of Orthodontics. Reception was negative. Most recognized leaders of that day said it wouldn't work.

In time, the impact of these prefabricated devices on the world of orthodontics was dramatic. Simply put, they changed the face of dentistry. The wide variety of appliance shapes and sizes supplied by RMO enabled orthodontists to treat a diverse array of patients more effectively.

"What was developed was a way of putting things together that provided more effective and creative options for doctors," says Martin Brusse, RMO chairman and chief executive officer, and son of the company's founder. "The orthodontist could employ a greater variety of different techniques through more individualized diagnosis and treatment. Patients would benefit."

These developments coincided with a period of significant progress in the science of bone biology and tooth movement, which was particularly beneficial to both RMO and the field of orthodontics overall. New studies

Rocky Mountain Orthodontics (RMO) maintains its role as an innovator and visionary, pushing the practice of orthodontics to new frontiers while continuing to provide a benchmark of quality for other companies to follow.

were revealing the long-term ineffectiveness of oral appliances that exceeded certain thresholds of pressure in moving teeth and resetting bites. Thus, a new mantra in orthodontics—"delicacy and strength"—was born. These two qualities perfectly characterized light, clean, versatile RMO appliance options.

Not only did Archie Brusse and his small staff turn a fledgling depression-time start-up business into a multimillion-dollar industry bellwether, but they also helped attract dentists to the practice of orthodontics by vastly improving the quality and diversity of tools available to them. By extension, RMO has made invaluable contributions that have improved the oral health and self-image of countless satisfied patients.

RMO was founded by Dr. Archie Brusse (left). His son, Martin Brusse (right), is the current chairman and CEO.

Setting the Standard

Today, RMO maintains its role as an innovator and visionary, pushing the practice of orthodontics to new frontiers while continuing to provide a benchmark of quality for other companies to follow. RMO's catalog now shows how 7,000 different basic products and services can be translated into a universe of treatment options for orthodontists all over the world.

Increasingly, RMO has emphasized the development of computer-aided diagnostic and treatment planning tools. These information innovations have provided powerful analytic information that has helped doctors and their staffs deal with each patient's individual growth and development. This results in fewer surprises and fewer after-orthodontics failures.

RMO's health care innovations have not gone unnoticed. RMO was awarded the prestigious E Award for excellence in educational marketing by two U.S. presidents, and the company has received the Colorado Governor's Award for consistent excellence in exporting.

These honors reflect RMO's status as a truly international company, with more than half of its revenue coming from outside the United States. RMO today maintains subsidiaries based in Strasbourg and Sydney, along with a 27-year-old joint venture relationship with the J. Morita Company in Japan. Sixty independent dental dealers in other countries round out a very impressive RMO global marketing effort.

Denver can be proud of the loyalty and efforts of the employees and the local commercial suppliers who have helped RMO succeed and advance during the company's history. RMO is, by all measures, an international standard bearer poised to build upon its legacy of excellence for decades to come.

The Phil Long Dealerships

The flight log for the USS *Enterprise*, the most decorated ship of World War II, records 126 takeoffs and 124 landings for Lieutenant Commander Philip Long. "I was shot down once and ran out of fuel the other time," says Long, whose matter-of-fact explanation reconciles the flight log, but understates the talents of one of Colorado Springs' most respected businessmen. Shortly after being discharged in September 1945, Long sold his first automobile at Doenges-Long Motors, which had been started earlier that year by this father. Long eventually bought the business in 1963 and changed the name to Phil Long Ford.

Colorado Springs was growing and Long had a vision to grow; thus, America's first auto mall was born in Colorado Springs on an 11-acre site on Motor City Drive. The mall was the first of several successful ventures calculated to expand the presence of Phil Long Ford in Colorado Springs.

The company grew during the next 12 years, and then, in 1975, Jay Cimino became a partner and general manager; Cimino now serves as company CEO. In 1976, Cimino hired Bob Fenton, who has subsequently become a partner and the general manager of Phil Long Ford of Motor City and Phil Long Ford of Chapel Hills. Jim Fynes, general manager of Phil Long Ford of Denver, and Marvin Boyd, COO of the Phil Long Dealerships, are also partners in the firm.

More than 50 years ago, Doenges-Long Motors—today known as the Phil Long Dealerships—established itself as a market leader through its commitment to providing value and excellent customer service.

Backed by an outstanding team of automotive, business, and financial professionals, Philip Long (left) and Jay Cimino have created the Phil Long Dealerships, the largest family of dealerships in Colorado.

Exponential Growth

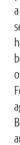his visionary team has accomplished much. Having begun as a modest company that conducted business with a handful of employees on south Nevada Avenue in 1945, the Phil Long Dealerships has become today the 33rd-largest dealership group in the United States and a member of the elite Fortune 500. With more than 1,500 employees and gross sales of nearly $580 million, the Phil Long Dealerships is the fifth-largest privately held corporation in Colorado. Over the years, the company has received numerous industry awards for record-breaking sales, superior customer service, and innovative design and presentation, as well as for its state-of-the-art facilities for parts and service.

Today, the company consists of 16 dealerships representing 12 manufacturers: Ford, Mercedes-Benz, Saturn, Jeep, Chrysler, Plymouth, Mitsubishi, Suzuki, Nissan, Hyundai, KIA, and Audi. This well-planned expansion was the result of careful market study and informed response to consumer demand.

The Phil Long Dealerships navigates the crosscurrents of consumer preferences by offering numerous automotive brands, which target a variety of customer wants and needs. Phil Long customers can choose from the largest vehicle inventory in the state of Colorado. However, competition in this industry is still fierce because today's consumers have access to a variety of local dealerships and many electronic shopping options provided by the Internet.

Tough markets force businesses to play to their strengths. The strength of the Phil Long Dealerships is its commitment to providing its customers with excellent service and value. For many consumers, the two are one and the same. Well-treated customers return to purchase again, and refer their relatives and friends. With more than 55 years in business, the Phil Long Dealerships has more than 2 million satisfied customers—an enviable situation wrought of longtime and painstaking attention to customer needs. Correctly discerning those needs has generated annual sales of about 25,000 retail vehicles per year.

Knowing What the Customer Wants

It pays to know what customers want. For those who do not want to negotiate the price of a car, Phil Long has pioneered a no-hassle alternative with ValuCAR. ValuCAR is currently one of the largest used-car superstores in America. The price is low, the price is fixed, and the price is usually right, given the satisfaction of thousands of Phil Long customers, who also appreciate that each pre-owned vehicle passed a 150-point mechanical and safety checklist prior to sale.

Some prospective buyers want access to as much information as possible without having to go to a dealership. The Phil Long Dealerships has met this demand by creating phillong.com, a Web site offering consumers access to Colorado's largest inventory of new and pre-owned vehicles. The site accommodates buyers who want to browse, research, or shop on the Internet because of the convenience and anonymity it offers. A recent sale to a customer from Maine, who flew out to Colorado Springs to pick up the vehicle he found and ordered on phillong.com, validates the Phil Long Dealerships' commitment to

excellence and superior customer service— even across the country.

Cimino considers Phil Long employees to be "dedicated experts at solving problems and satisfying customers," and nothing is more essential in the hypercompetitive automotive market. To ensure that all employees receive formal, ongoing training, the company developed Phil Long University (PLU), an innovative, in-house program that addresses the specific needs of each job classification in the company, from sales to clerical to technical personnel. PLU's mission is employee excellence, and the payoff has been better-educated, more productive employees with higher morale resulting from the company's visible investment in their career development. Perhaps the most telling sign of PLU's success has been the attention the program

has received from other dealerships seeking to learn more about Phil Long's features.

For decades, the Phil Long Dealerships has supported its local communities with contributions of money, product, time, and labor. In 1991, the company formalized its commitment to civic responsibility by founding the Phil Long Community Fund, a private foundation that champions the self-esteem and performance of youth in sports, education, and recreation. The fund recognizes that an investment in youth is an investment in the communities that have contributed to the continued success of the Phil Long Dealerships. Since its inception, the fund has helped thousands of children by giving more than $600,000 to nonprofit organizations in Colorado Springs and Denver, including Junior Achievement, the YMCA, and the Denver Zoo.

The Phil Long Community Fund's largest project is the annual funding of community-built playgrounds in the Colorado Springs and Denver metro areas. In partnership with the Denver Broncos Charity Fund, the Phil Long Community Fund has allocated thousands of dollars since 1995 to subsidize these community projects, the most recent of which have been the Phil Long/Denver Broncos Community Playground located in Colorado Springs' Memorial Park, completed in September 1999, and the Knapp Elementary Playground in Denver, completed in September 2000.

The Phil Long Dealerships benefits from and contributes to the economic growth and well-being of the communities it serves. For more than half a century, the company has striven to meet the needs of its customers and their communities. Long's vision and remarkable talents have produced long-term corporate and social benefits: greater employment, increased prosperity, advantaged youth, and a healthier community.

The Phil Long Community Fund/Denver Broncos Charity Fund Community Playground in Colorado Springs' Memorial Park is one example of the Phil Long Dealerships' dedication to improving the communities that have contributed to the company's success.

When Denver's oil industry boomed in the 1970s, the *Denver Business Journal* was there to report the success; when oil went bust in the 1980s, the weekly was there to report the failure. From stories of cable cowboys to the discoveries of biotech pioneers, the *Denver Business Journal* has stayed atop Denver's business community since 1948. ●

"We're the oldest weekly business publication in the United States," says Publisher Scott Bemis, who celebrated the *Denver Business Journal's* 50th anniversary in 1998. "We concentrate primarily on the metro area and that's the great value we offer. You're reading about yourself, your neighbors, your customers, and your companies, rather than trying to be statewide."

To be all-business and all-local is the byword of American City Business Journals Inc., the nation's largest publisher of metropolitan business newspapers. American City Business Journals owns the *Denver Business Journal* and 40 other papers in the nation's most vital markets.

Getting Down to Business

Founded by Denver's legendary newspaper curmudgeon Gene Cervi in September 1948, the *Denver Business Journal* has grown to a circulation of nearly 15,000 and a total readership of 100,000. The newspaper employs some 36 people, including some 13 in the editorial department. Readers have an average individual salary of $144,000, an average household income of $201,000, and an average net worth of $1.4 million. Approximately 36 percent of the *Denver Business Journal's* readers are millionaires.

"Seventy percent of our readers are in top and middle management positions; they need to be in the know and must subscribe," says Bemis, who points out that readership among women also is growing. "Seventeen years ago, 8 percent of our readers were women. We are now at 32 percent."

The *Denver Business Journal* emphasizes small-business coverage in a state where more than 95 percent of businesses are considered small business. *Denver Business Journal* readership reflects this trend, with 58 percent of subscribing companies having revenues less than $4.9 million.

Besides publishing a weekly paper that includes such regular features as *Strategies* and *Names in the News*, and special sections on real estate, high-tech, professional services, marketing, and selling tips, the *Denver Business Journal* publishes the *Who's Who* and the *Book of Lists* annually. The *Denver Business Journal* also produces several business-to-business events each year to recognize achievements: Deal Makers, which recognizes the biggest and best deals in Denver business; Top 150, which highlights the area's fastest-growing private companies; Outstanding Women in Business, honoring successful businesswomen; and Colorado's Most Innovative New Products. New events include Groundbreakers, honoring those who have built new projects in the Denver area, and Top 100 Public Companies, honoring companies for their growth, as well as for largest IPOs, CEO of the Year, and community involvement.

"We've drawn nearly 400 people for every event," says Bemis. "This is our way of bringing businesspeople together to honor them for various achievements. That is what the *Denver Business Journal* has always stood for: covering the business landscape, staying local, and staying on top of what is going on in the metro area."

Besides publishing a weekly paper that includes such regular features as *Strategies* and *Names in the News*, and special sections on real estate, high-tech, professional services, marketing, and selling tips, the *Denver Business Journal* publishes the *Who's Who* and the *Book of Lists* annually.

Readership of the *Denver Business Journal* is growing, especially among women, who currently comprise 32 percent of the readers.

Nestled in the heart of Denver's unique Cherry Creek shopping district is Foster and Son jewelers, a local fixture since its opening in 1959. For more than 40 years, this store has not only provided quality jewelry, but also developed a reputation for integrity and excellent customer service. In a testament to the owners' commitment to these ideas, the company is now serving its fourth generation of Colorado customers. ● "We are blessed with our longevity," says Brien Foster, who, along with his wife, Cindi, continues the Foster tradition. "Little babies who used to come in here with their parents are now coming to us as young adults for their engagement rings."

A Family Affair

Originally called the 14 Karat, the shop was opened in 1959 by Foster's mother, the late Patricia Foster. A single mother of three who had spent years in jewelry merchandising, she broke into the traditionally male-dominated jewelry business by specializing in solid gold jewelry.

"Her amazing sense of organization, her charming personality, her business sense, and a bit of luck all made her a success," says Brien Foster. He was able to join his mother in the business in 1975 at a 500-square-foot shop on Second Avenue, which served as her third location.

Brien Foster was a natural for the jewelry business, venturing into the industry while in the navy in Memphis, where he worked part-time for a jeweler. After his discharge, Foster apprenticed at a manufacturing jeweler in New York; LaVake Jewelers in Princeton, New Jersey; and Vance Boyd Jewelers in Memphis.

When Foster came home to Denver, the 14 Karat company name was changed to Foster and Son to celebrate the mother-son partnership and reflect the store's growing jewelry collection. The particular niche of solid gold jewelry that prompted the store's success allowed it to expand and grow over the years. Upon his mother's retirement in 1987, Foster bought Foster and Son to ensure the family-owned company would continue the traditions upon which it was founded.

"We have wonderful customers who are loyal to us and who make each day a new experience," says Foster. "I've been in the jewelry business for 30 years—25 of those years have been with Foster and Son—and I can't think of anything I'd rather do. It's a fun business because you're dealing with people who are doing nice things for one another."

Brien and Cindi Foster have two young sons they hope may someday continue the Foster family legacy. Patricia Foster died in 1991, leaving behind her own special words to live by: "Never forget the lost virtue of earning trust and confidence. Be simple. Have integrity, value, and that special personal touch of service." This philosophy is what Foster and Son adheres to today.

Foster and Son is currently owned by Brien Foster and his wife Cindi.

Bill McGuckin, an avid fisherman who enjoyed the Colorado outdoors, opened McGuckin Hardware in 1955. His eclectic career path took him from a job at a pharmacy to a Colorado oil field where he leased the land, and finally to the venerable hardware store that still bears his name. ● McGuckin founded the modest business at a time when Boulder stretched east only as far as Folsom Street and when Arapahoe Avenue was the lone route to Denver. In the beginning, there were only four employees working in four departments in the little shop on the north side of Arapahoe Avenue.

McGuckin carried mostly nuts and bolts, plus a few sporting goods.

Over time, McGuckin learned that it took more than nuts and bolts to run a successful retail operation. It took good customer service and a belief that when customers needed something, he would get it for them.

McGuckin died in 1966, but his dedication to personalized service and firsthand experience lives on. "We're still doing all those things more than 40 years later," says David Hight, McGuckin's son-in-law, who became a partner in McGuckin Hardware in 1960. "We believe in offering customers personal service, and always have what they want. If we don't, we order it for them or make suggestions on what else they might use."

Today, McGuckin Hardware is still a family-run business. Now in his seventies, Hight still comes in every day and works the floor as a sales clerk, among other duties. His three sons—Barry, Brent, and Rob—all worked in McGuckin when they were growing up. Today, Barry Hight is president. "He couldn't wait until he could see over the cash register so he could work in the store," David Hight says.

McGuckin Hardware's east entrance is colorfully accented by one of the many inspiring flower gardens that give the neighborhood a homey feel.

McGuckin's vast 60,000-square-foot showroom holds nearly 300,000 items.

The World's Largest Hardware Selection

McGuckin Hardware has grown significantly from its early days, now carrying nearly 300,000 items purchased from more than 5,000 vendors. "We're known to have the world's largest hardware selection, and we try not to tell anybody we don't have something," says Hight. McGuckin today has 18 departments, from automotive, bolts, builder's hardware, electrical, electronics, hobbies, housewares, fireplaces, sporting goods, pets, and greenery, to tools, garden center, paints, plumbing equipment, seasonal, stationery, and outdoor living. More than 300 highly trained employees, all wearing McGuckin signature green vests, work on the 60,000-plus-square-foot sales floor.

The store is renowned for stocking obscure specialty items that few other retailers carry. Its staff is famous for special-ordering unusual items that customers seek, and has even been known to fabricate an item to solve a customer's hardware problem.

"There's a lot of knowledge on our sales floor," says Hight. "Knowledge is where it all is and sets us apart from the big stores. No one is more knowledgeable about what we carry than the buyers and the people on the floor."

At McGuckin, customers also find variety. While the store originally carried only one kind of glue, today's McGuckin stocks 200 types. In addition, in a snow state like Colorado, McGuckin offers 30 kinds of snow shovels.

"We really want to cater to every one of our customers so we offer all different kinds of things," says Hight. "Retail is so exciting today because we have so many good products available."

A Growing Business

McGuckin Hardware has moved several times since its founding, but never more than a few blocks from the site of the original store. In 1976,

McGuckin moved to its present home. In the last few years, the store has expanded, maintaining a modern look on the outside but an old-fashioned feel on the inside.

McGuckin also has expanded beyond its Arapahoe Avenue setting, opening a satellite business in Boulder. At McGuckin Design Center on Canyon Boulevard, six experienced designers assist customers with their kitchen and bathroom designs. The Design Center also features hardware, cabinets, plumbing fixtures, and door hardware.

Calling Colorado Home

The McGuckin reputation is so well known that even Hollywood celebrities have stopped by while in Colo-rado. Bing Crosby came in while filming *Stagecoach,* Jane Fonda shopped in the housewares department while visiting her son at the University of Colorado, and Bill Murray and Eddie Murphy cut up while browsing the aisles during a break in filming a movie.

A visitor to Boulder from Paris was so pleased with the store that he vowed to build one in Paris. Today, there is a McGuckin copycat hardware store in Paris. A business-man visiting IBM went back to Tokyo and built a similar store there.

"We encourage everyone to build stores like this," says Hight. "We've been asked to franchise, but we always say no. I would rather see individual families build their own stores. That way you have several different families each making a living from their businesses."

Like its founder, the store calls Colorado home and serves its people with the utmost care and consideration, and the people of the state have responded warmly. The *Daily Camera* awarded McGuckin two Best of Boulder awards in 1999—and again in 2000—one for Best Service and one for Best Hard-ware Store.

From its beginnings as a small shop offer-ing only the essentials to a one-stop shop for every hardware need, McGuckin has remained loyal to its founder's vision and dedication to personal service. Customers can be sure that McGuckin Hardware will continue to work toward these ideals for decades to come.

The easy-to-navigate aisles at McGuckin Hardware are marked with letters and numbers on the floor, so customers can quickly find what they need. In addition, large green signs with easy-to-read white lettering indicate the locations of the various store departments.

Two Boulder attractions: The famous Flatirons provide a fitting backdrop for McGuckin Hardware's north entrance.

Denver Broncos Football Club

For the better part of four decades, the Denver Broncos Football Club has been the heart and soul of Denver. From the first nationally televised Monday night game in 1973, through 26 postseason games that have included six Super Bowl appearances and back-to-back world championships, the Broncos arguably have provided the Mile High City's primary identity on a national and international level. ● The Broncos, Denver's first major-league team, began play in 1960 as a charter member of the new American Football League. The team was sold the next year to Rocky Mountain Empire Sports, a syndicate headed by Gerald and Allan Phipps. In 1965, the Phipps family became the team's sole owner.

Ownership of the Broncos passed to Edgar Kaiser in 1981 and, three years later, to current owner Pat Bowlen. Bowlen, a businessman with interests in oil, gas, and real estate, and an avid amateur athlete in his own right, is actively involved in the team's day-to-day operations as president and chief executive officer. Widely praised throughout the National Football League (NFL) as a dynamic chief executive, Bowlen has stamped the Broncos as a dominant team in the American Football Conference Western Division (AFC West).

Today, the Broncos organization operates from the Paul D. Bowlen Memorial Broncos Centre, located on 13.5 acres of land in the Dove Valley Business Park in southern Arapahoe County. The Denver Broncos Football Club employs about 150 people full-time.

The Denver Broncos Football Club has called Mile High Stadium home since 1960. In 2001, the Broncos will celebrate the opening season of a brand-new stadium.

With $75 million in annual revenues, the organization is one of Denver's top 50 private companies.

An Elite Organization

...ed by future Hall of Fame quarterback John Elway, the Broncos won consecutive Super Bowls in 1997 and 1998. The team also established all-time pro football records for most wins in two seasons (33), most playoff wins in two seasons (seven), and most wins ever in three seasons (46, from 1996 through 1998)—all records that will be very difficult to challenge.

The club played its first winning season in 1973, which also was the year of its first nationally televised game. Since then, the team has helped focus the attention of the nation and the world on Denver. Televised Broncos games from Denver offer the entire nation incredible vistas of the Rocky Mountains. When it snows during a televised home game, out-of-state calls for reservations at the state's ski resorts jump 50 percent.

In 1977, a defense comprised of five pro bowl players—known collectively as the Orange Crush—propelled the Denver Broncos to the team's first Super Bowl game, validating the faith of the team's loyal fans. In 1983, Elway joined the team, the first player taken in that year's NFL draft.

During the 1980s, the Denver Broncos became the only AFC club to appear in three Super Bowls. The team has won two world championships, played in a total of six Super Bowls, made seven AFC championship game appearances, and won nine AFC West titles.

An internationally popular team, the Denver Broncos Football Club has represented

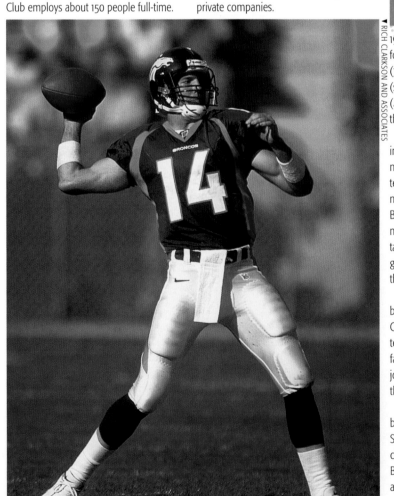

The Broncos have established all-time pro football records for most wins in two seasons (33), most play-off wins in two seasons (seven), and most wins ever in three seasons (46, from 1996 through 1998)—all records that will be very difficult to challenge.

Capacity was doubled in 1960 for the Broncos' first season.

In 1967, voters declined a bond issue to construct a new stadium, but fans came to the rescue. Forming a nonprofit group—called the DOERS—they raised $1.8 million to purchase Bears Stadium from its private owners; the DOERS then presented the deed to the city. An upper deck that increased capacity to 50,000 was added the following year, and the facility was renamed Denver Mile High Stadium. In 1971, voters approved a $25 million bond issue to expand the stadium to more than 75,000 seats.

The capacity of Mile High Stadium now stands at 76,082, making it one of the largest facilities in the NFL. At more than 50 years of age, it is also the oldest stadium in the NFL, hosting more pro football games than any other currently occupied stadium. In 2001, Denver and the Broncos will celebrate the opening season of a brand-new stadium— one that will provide the ultimate football experience for players and spectators alike, and a facility that will be worthy of the entire state's pride. The new stadium assures a prominent place for Denver as professional football moves into the 21st century.

From the first nationally televised Monday night game in 1973, through 26 postseason games that have included six Super Bowl appearances and back-to-back world championships, the Broncos arguably have provided the Mile High City's primary identity on a national and international level.

the NFL, Denver, and the region in seven American Bowl games since 1987, playing in London, Berlin, Barcelona, Tokyo (twice), Mexico City, and Sydney.

In 1993, the Denver Broncos cheerleading squad made its popular debut after an absence of 17 years. The team's mascot, Thunder, a purebred white Arabian stallion, also debuted that year.

The Love of a Frontier Town

Denver fans' devotion to the Broncos stands out even in a city with strong loyalty to its other teams. The team has enjoyed some 30 consecutive sellout

seasons, dating back to 1969, and the highest local television ratings of any NFL city during that time.

Denver's love affair and support of the Broncos helped attract other professional teams here, but the term "Broncomania" was born out of the genuine fanaticism surrounding pro football in the Mile High City. The city's collective Monday morning psyche often appears to hinge on how well its team did that previous Sunday.

The team has always played in Mile High Stadium. The stadium originally was built in 1948 for the city's minor-league baseball team, the Denver Bears, with a capacity of 18,000.

1961-1980

1963	Alpine Lumber Company
1967	Community Colleges of Colorado
1970	Kodak Colorado
1975	Marriott
1975	Radisson Stapleton Plaza
1977	Durrant
1977	HenryGill Advertising
1980	People's Choice Transportation
1980	S. A. Miro, Inc.
1980	TRW Inc.

Founded as a single lumberyard in Englewood, Colorado, in 1963, Alpine Lumber Company is today one of the largest and geographically broadest suppliers of lumber and building materials in the state. ● Alpine's vast inventory of building materials mainly goes into new residential construction—everything from starter homes and tract homes to multimillion-dollar luxury mountain homes in the ski towns of Telluride and Steamboat Springs. "We're comfortable supplying materials to build any level of home," says Kip Oram, president. "We work in partnership with our customers, the home builders, to provide the best service possible. We like to think of ourselves as offering small lumberyard service with big lumberyard clout."

Serving Colorado

The company maintains eight retail yards and three wholesale and support operations, serving such diverse markets as Denver, Frederick, Granby, Loveland, Montrose, Parker, Steamboat Springs, and Telluride. The yard in Frederick opened in March 2000, a welcome new business at the heart of Colorado's growth.

Alpine also maintains a retail building materials bargain outlet, as well as several wholesale and specialty support operations, including two prehung door shops and two window and cabinet distribution and service facilities. In addition, the company has a materials takeoff and engineered-floor systems design center and a complete, rail-serviced reload facility, as well as Alpine Truss Co. in Brighton.

"Our eight lumber yards could not be more different from each other," says Bob Curran, sales manager. "Our managers operate them as entrepreneurs. They have goals and guidelines, but day-to-day operations are based on what works for them. That way, we can react quickly to the needs of our customers in a specific market; we don't have to call a committee meeting to get things accomplished."

Each builder-oriented lumberyard has its own professional staff and a product mix unique to the market, whether it means supplying materials for the high-end homes in the mountains or for the family homes on the Colorado Plains.

Alpine Lumber Company President Kip Oram encourages an entrepreneurial approach to management and insists that operational flexibility be maintained at the individual locations.

With construction no longer a purely seasonal endeavor, Alpine's new yards have been designed for optimum efficiency under any weather conditions.

Working with the Building Community

In the midst of Colorado's building boom, a shortage of labor has become the norm. The builders' response has been to establish predictable production time lines, and then to shorten them as much as possible. Alpine's part in this is to deliver precisely what the builder wants exactly when it is wanted. "Ten o'clock in the morning does not mean eight and it does not mean noon," says Curran. "Skilled people are scarce and expensive, and the builder needs them working, not waiting."

Alpine has no illusions about its role; the company exists to service the builder. The advent of big-box retailers, formatted operations, and national chain consolidations has only served to strengthen the level of commitment. "There are a lot of folks out there who will tell you they've figured out how to sell to professionals and do-it-yourselfers from the same facility," says Curran. "In my opinion, they're full of something other than good ideas."

A Commitment to Its Employees

Much of the way Alpine does business stems from the fact that, since 1989, the company has been 100 percent employee-owned. The founding Kurtz family created an employee stock ownership plan (ESOP) and turned the company over to the employees, who are eligible to participate

after just one year on the job. Pride of ownership among Alpine's employees runs deep throughout the company.

"We have been fortunate as a company that when the Colorado economy was suffering, there were overqualified people whom we were actually able to hire and put in a truck or take on as a cashier, and they stayed with us," says Oram. "It meant long hours of hard work and it had little prestige value. But all promotions come from within, so it's essential that we retain people. With our sense of ownership, people do stay and move up in the company."

Alpine's financial picture is impressive as well. Since, 1991, the company has averaged 15 to 20 percent annual growth, breaking the $20 million sales mark in 1992. Sales projections for 2000 were put at $120 million.

In 1999, *Colorado Biz* magazine ranked Alpine Lumber the 32nd-largest private company in Colorado, while the *Denver*

Business Journal ranked it 27th. The trade publication *Pro Dealer* named Alpine the 42nd-largest contractor supplier nationally. More growth is on the way.

"We've gotten together with some key employee stockholders to do some strategic planning, and their wish is to continue to grow and expand as quickly as we have been doing," says Oram. "The timing could not have been better with the building boom as it is."

A Civic-Minded Company

Managers at each Alpine lumberyard determine charitable giving and company participation in community projects. On a company level, civic-minded Alpine backed a statewide campaign for the Colorado chapter of the Nature Conservancy. "We're hunters and fishermen and hikers," says Oram. "We're as much conservationists as anyone else in this state."

Alpine also worked with the Home Build-

ers Foundation of Metropolitan Denver to renovate the homes of three shooting victims of the Columbine High School tragedy to make them wheelchair accessible.

"Alpine is a rare example of a civic-minded Colorado success story driven by a nice earthy attitude led by a nice group of top management," writes Jeff Whiton, president of the Home Builders Foundation, in *Home Builder Magazine.*

**Clockwise from top left:
Manager Dan Taggart directs the efforts at Alpine Lumber's newest yard in Frederick, Colorado. This yard will serve the busy area north of Metro Denver.**

Top-notch facilities and equipment are a necessity, but in the lumber business the people still do the work and the people still make the difference.

Outbound "built loads" are staged and ready for delivery when the builder calls. The first item needed is on the top, the last on the bottom.

Almost all long-term Alpine employees have experience in every phase of lumberyard operations and can quickly shift to where they are needed. In a busy yard, multitasking is essential.

Community Colleges of Colorado

Community Colleges of Colorado (CC of C) is the state's largest and fastest-growing institution of higher education, serving some 250,000 Coloradans each year through 14 state system community colleges, two local district community colleges, four area vocational schools, and career/technical programs in 150 school districts. Each college offers a blend of core courses for the university bound, as well as career programs that meet the workforce needs of the burgeoning dot-com economy.

A Cohesive System of Education

The fully accredited, comprehensive two-year community colleges that make up this system include Arapahoe Community College in Littleton; Colorado Northwestern Community College in Rangely; Community College of Aurora; Community College of Denver; Front Range Community College in Westminster; Lamar Community College; Morgan Community College in Fort Morgan; Northeastern Junior College in Sterling; Otero Junior College in La Junta; Pikes Peak Community College in Colorado Springs; Pueblo Community College; Red Rocks Community College in Lakewood; and Trinidad State Junior College. Aims and Colorado Mountain College, in Greeley and Glenwood Springs, respectively, are the local district community colleges.

The common thread that has pulled CC of C together into a cohesive system of education is the commitment to providing educational opportunity to all of Colorado's citizens. The institution's early growth was fueled by the civil rights movement, returning Vietnam veterans, and the baby boomers and their children. Today, new social, demographic, and economic changes are multipliers. Federal Reserve Chairman Alan Greenspan has observed, "Because of the tightness of the labor markets, the value of on-the-job training and the remarkable expansion in community colleges have had a major positive effect on our workforce." In its most recent year, CC of C enrolled 247,289 students, some two-thirds of whom are training for specific jobs and careers.

Community Colleges of Colorado offers more than 450 programs that prepare students for careers in such diverse fields as health care, advanced manufacturing, zoology, and aviation. New e-commerce offerings are attracting small-business people from across the state. And at the Higher Education and Advanced Technologies (HEAT) Center at Lowry, state-of-the-practice education in high-tech fields is coupled with research on how best to teach and learn in the Knowledge Age.

Accessible Opportunity

CC of C has an extensive track record. The organization serves six out of 10 public college freshmen and sophomores in Colorado, and provides customized training to more than 40,000 employees of some 3,000 businesses annually. Community Colleges of Colorado plays a major role in training the workforce for Colorado's robust economy, as well as preparing myriad university-bound students for four-year studies.

Clockwise from top right:
Students at Community Colleges of Colorado (CC of C) increasingly have their eyes on computers as a way to access college courses and technology as a key to their careers.

CC of C offers programs from aviation to zoology, including more than 450 different programs at 14 colleges.

CC of C helps students bridge the gaps in their lives with anytime, anywhere learning.

Founded in Denver in 1980 as a van and limousine operation, People's Choice Transportation has become Colorado's largest locally owned motor coach company. With new ownership coming on board in 1992, the company has grown to a 56-vehicle fleet in 2000. The firm operates Colorado's newest fleet of radio-dispatched vehicles, including deluxe motor coaches that each carry 47 to 55 passengers, minibuses that transport 24 passengers, and 14-passenger vans. In all, the vehicles logged more than 4 million miles in 2000. ●"This is a very challenging business," says Joanne Lah,

president of People's Choice. "We have experienced a 106 percent growth in the last eight years, and with that comes growing pains. Because we have a dedicated, hardworking team, we have moved to the forefront of the motor coach industry here in the West. Denver's being such a great place to live or visit has helped give us the opportunity to expand."

The company's performance has attracted the attention of those outside the industry, with *Colorado Business Magazine* in 1998 naming People's Choice one of the top 100 woman-owned businesses in Colorado, and one of the top 250 companies in Colorado in 1999. Lah, who employs some 130 people, is one of only a few women across the nation to head a motor coach business.

Developing New Transport Venues

People's Choice grew out of the introduction of gaming to Colorado, but today relies on that industry for only a portion of its market. Uniformed, professional drivers safely navigate curvy mountain roads while gamblers sit back and enjoy the scenery. The company operates more than 90 daily departures to the gambling towns of Black Hawk and Central City.

In addition to its scheduled service, People's Choice has a thriving charter business. "We

have worked diligently to diversify, and that's what makes our operation so successful," says Lah. The company works with corporate clients, as well as tour operators, meeting planners, school districts, sporting events, the military, and family charters—in other words, anyone who needs group transportation.

Top-Notch Service

We provide a luxury charter service to our clients, and that sets us apart," says Lah, adding that the company has seen many different trends in the market. "We constantly strive to be ahead of the pack; this is a competitive

market and we work hard to stay on top."

World events often touch the company at its headquarters just outside Denver. People's Choice has provided transportation for the Secret Service during a visit by Former President Bill Clinton, as well as for the Summit of the Eight conference of world leaders and the Chinese delegation. Colorado's governor and Denver's mayor also use People's Choice for their transportation needs.

In order to provide quality service, the company employs a skilled maintenance crew to keep its fleet in top shape, and a detail crew that makes sure the vehicles are always spotless. People's Choice has an outstanding sales staff, with more than 50 collective years' experience in the industry. The company's professional drivers receive constant training and education to keep them at the top. "Our strong safety and training program regularly receives the highest ratings from state and federal regulatory agencies," says Lah. "We work hard to provide a good product, knowing it takes premier people to make a premier company. We have that, and because of it, we truly believe the sky is the limit for us."

People's Choice Transportation operates Colorado's newest fleet of radio-dispatched vehicles, including deluxe motor coaches that each carry 47 to 55 passengers, minibuses that transport 24 passengers, and 14-passenger vans.

Kodak Colorado

Picture this: major manufacturing buildings housing 1,800 employees and situated on 2,200 panoramic acres. A bike path winds through the site along a picturesque river. Bald eagles, deer, and indigenous plants all reside here.

● This is not a Hollywood set, but a snapshot of Kodak Colorado—a division of the Rochester, New York-based Eastman Kodak Co.—which in 1970 began manufacturing a variety of photographic films and papers in Windsor, Colorado. About 40 people work in Kodak Colorado's motion picture and television film finishing department. Some of the film is used by

Hollywood, as blockbuster movies are wound on reels and sent to movie theaters around the globe.

But Kodak Colorado's primary mission is the manufacture of medical X-ray film, including most of the film used for lifesaving mammograms that detect breast cancer. "We do quite a bit for our employees during the month of October, which is a time dedicated to finding a cure for breast cancer," says Lucille Mantelli, spokeswoman for Kodak Colorado. "Among other things, we give ribbons to all our employees in recognition of the Race for the Cure, and, when available, bring in a mobile mammography unit that offers free mammograms."

The founding of Kodak Colorado came about after officials in Rochester combed the Midwest and Far West in search of a place to build its new facility. After three years, company management decided on Windsor—with its expansive site, quality water supply, nearby universities, excellent workforce, and attractive neighboring communities—as the perfect site for Kodak Colorado.

Eastman Kodak was growing, diversifying, and focusing on staying abreast of technologies when it constructed nine major manufacturing buildings on 600 of Kodak Colorado's 2,200 acres. This left ample opportunity for future expansion.

The facility is a site Eastman Kodak founder George Eastman could only have dreamed about when he introduced his first Kodak

camera in 1888 and began his lifelong pursuit of making photography available to everyone.

Applying New Technologies

Kodak's technology goes beyond photos and cameras. Thermal media manufacturing, for example, is the newest technological catchphrase at Kodak Colorado. This process entails the manufacture of cellophane ribbons that allow printers to duplicate prints from optical scanners, photo CDs, or other computer-based image generators. Currently, the ribbons are being

used in photocopying machines such as those found in drugstores and grocery stores.

Sensitizing, too, is a technology at the heart of Kodak Colorado's operations. Photographic film is born here when a coat of light-sensitive emulsion is applied to the bases of large rolls of film. Photographic paper for snapshots, portraits, or enlargements is made in the facility's Sensitizing Complex, which consists of four manufacturing buildings. In addition, Kodak Colorado produces ink-jet paper for color printers, which photographers use to print out photos taken with digital cameras. "Our business remains

Clockwise from top:
Kodak Colorado is situated on 2,200 panoramic acres in Windsor, Colorado.

Thermal media manufacturing is the newest technological advancement at Kodak Colorado. This process entails the manufacture of cellophane ribbons that allow printers to duplicate prints from optical scanners, photo CDs, or other computer-based image generators.

Kodak Colorado's primary mission is the manufacture of medical X-ray film, including most of the film used for lifesaving mammograms that detect breast cancer.

stable here and our consumer-imaging film production continues to grow," says Mantelli.

Kodak Colorado is one of Colorado's largest exporters, sending myriad products from its 435,000-square-foot, temperature-controlled distribution center directly to foreign markets. Fleets of trucks and railcars move the company's products across the United States and around the world.

Preserving the Environment

Kodak Colorado also has a strong environmental focus, with 400 acres set aside for wildlife preservation. Company landscapers built nests for geese, and planted a variety of shrubs and trees to provide food and shelter for the wildlife that inhabit the area or migrate annually. Another 3.2-mile stretch of land, donated to the Poudre River Trail system, is now being used as a bike trail.

"We also lease 40 acres along the Cache la Poudre River to the Colorado Division of Wildlife for use as a Watchable Wildlife Area," says Mantelli. "It's open from sunup to sundown. Every Earth Day, we bring area seventh graders to the wildlife area to learn about such things as the velocity of the stream, raptors, or the scope of the river."

An additional 1,500 acres are leased for farming and grazing in the heart of rural Colorado, where major crops include barley, alfalfa, corn, sugar beets, and pinto beans.

Supporting the Community

While the company has changed significantly since Eastman's 1880s heyday, Kodak's commitment to community remains strong, with an emphasis on local giving. In northern Colorado, the company supports the Weld County, Fort Collins, and Loveland/Berthoud United Way campaigns.

Kodak Colorado officials serve on several boards, including an advisory board for Colorado State University's mechanical engineering department. The company also is active in northern Colorado chambers of commerce, economic development programs, hospitals, high schools, the American Heart Association, and the American Cancer Society.

"We're very active in the community, giving $375,000 annually—primarily to the northern Colorado communities of Loveland, Greeley, Windsor, and Fort Collins," says Mantelli. "We believe it is important to be involved in the community that supports us so much."

Eastman, who as a young man in the 1870s began inventing at his mother's sink, likely would be proud of the Kodak legacy in Windsor, Colorado.

Clockwise from top left:
Kodak Colorado is one of Colorado's largest exporters, sending myriad products from its 435,000-square-foot, temperature-controlled distribution center directly to foreign markets.

Kodak's consumer products turn moments into everlasting memories.

Kodak Colorado has a strong environmental focus, with 400 acres set aside for wildlife preservation. The company also brings area seventh graders to the wildlife area to learn about such things as the velocity of the stream, raptors, and the scope of the river.

Marriott International, Inc.

In 1975, Denver became home to the first of a growing number of Marriott International, Inc. properties. Being the home away from home for countless tourists and businesspeople who, over the decades, have helped shape Colorado's thriving economy, the facilities of Marriott International have also shaped the area. Marriott International is a leading worldwide hospitality company, employing some 3,000 in the Denver market and 151,000 worldwide, with a portfolio of well-known lodging brands. Marriott Lodging operates and franchises hotels under the Marriott, Renaissance, Residence Inn, Courtyard, TownePlace Suites, Fairfield Inn, SpringHill Suites, and Ramada International brand names. Vacation ownership resorts are developed and operated under the Marriott, Ritz-Carlton, and Horizons brands; long-term-stay business apartments are operated by Marriott Executive Apartments; furnished corporate housing is provided through the ExecuStay by Marriott division; and conference centers are operated throughout the properties. Other Marriott businesses include senior living communities and services, wholesale food distribution, procurement services, and the Ritz-Carlton Hotel Company LLC.

History in Denver

The Fortune 500 Marriott International has more than 25 years in its history in the Denver area, where the company has an extensive commitment to developing its management team from the ground up. At least 72 percent of Marriott's managers started with the company as hourly employees and worked their way up through the ranks. Marriott International spends $100 million a year in training, which is a productivity tool as well as a retention tool that employees see as a pathway to new career opportunities and advancement.

That's the thinking of J.W. Marriott Jr., whose father and mother—J. Willard Marriott, a native of Utah, and his wife, Allie—founded the company in 1927. The senior Marriott launched the Marriott empire at the age of 26, opening a nine-seat root beer stand in Washington, D.C., that eventually grew into a restaurant chain, Hot Shoppes Inc., and the Marriott International that followed.

"For more than 70 years, we've lived by a simple motto: If we take care of our associates, they'll take care of the guest," says J.W. Marriott Jr., chairman and chief executive officer for Marriott International. "Marriott has enjoyed some success in recruiting and retaining associates. Our turnover rate is one of the lowest in the hospitality industry."

Marriott himself knows from personal experience the adage of "working your way up," having served in a number of capacities in his father's Hot Shoppes restaurant chain during his high school and college years, before joining the company full-time in 1956. Eight months later, he took over the company's Twin Bridges Motor Motel—Marriott's first venture into the lodging industry—in Washington, D.C., where the company's corporate headquarters is located today.

Guest and Industry Accolades

Marriott International regularly wins the accolades of its guests and others, with the year 2000 being a particularly good one for the hospitality giant with an eye for small details.

In October 2000, SmartMoney readers voted the company's flagship brand, Marriott Hotels, Resorts, and Suites, the best hotel brand in the magazine's first Have It Your Way Readers' Choice Awards. SmartMoney readers cited the friendly, caring, and service-focused associates who work at the brand's more than 370 hotels worldwide as a key factor in Marriott Hotels, Resorts, and Suites' earning top honors. When 600 randomly selected SmartMoney subscribers were polled, 28 percent identified overall quality of service as their deciding factor in choosing a hotel.

"It's a great honor to be recognized by SmartMoney readers," says Marriott. "It represents Marriott's ongoing commitment to anticipating the needs of the guest and placing a strong focus on providing the highest-quality service possible."

Marriott Hotels, Resorts, and Suites was also recognized for providing guests with high-speed Internet access, as well as At Your Service[SM], a service that provides guests with a personal liaison to address their needs—from business center services to driving directions, and from a wake-up call to room service. At Your Service is one of Marriott's six new Thinking of You guest services and brand enhancements.

Marriott Hotel City Center, a Marriott International, Inc. property, is conveniently located in downtown Denver.

Forbes ASAP also recognized Marriott International for its advances in technology, awarding the company four stars in its America's Best Technology Users list, noting the Marriott Automated Reservation System for Hotel Accommodations as the best software for filling rooms at optimal rates.

In another survey, J.D. Power and Associates awarded Courtyard by Marriott and Fairfield Inn top honors for customer satisfaction in the hotel industry for 2000. Marriott Rewards recently received the highest grade possible in the frequent travel program report card issued by BizTravel.com. On the site, travel guru Randy Petersen named Marriott Rewards class valedictorian, and praised the program's consistently superior performance, elite membership benefits, and ongoing Marriott/VISA Daily Double promotion.

Franchise Times magazine ranked Marriott Hotels, Resorts, and Suites eighth out of the world's top 200 franchise systems—the only hotel brand to make the top 10 list in the magazine's annual franchise report. In addition, Marriott had four other hotel brands in the top 100, including Courtyard, Renaissance, Residence Inn, and Fairfield Inn. Companies were judged on financial size and number of units. Marriott plans to manage or franchise a hotel in every gateway city in the world within the next five years. The company's goal is to reach 2,600 hotels and more than 480,000 rooms by 2003.

Employee Satisfaction

During the boom times of today's hot economy and the employee shortage that comes with it, Marriott International surveyed its employees about their employment and work environment and what mattered to them.

"Their top concern was indeed total compensation, but intangible factors taken together like work-life balance, leadership quality, opportunity for advancement, work environment, and training far outweighed money in their decisions to stay or leave," says Marriott. "We found that the longer an associate is with us, pay matters less and these factors matter more."

The company regularly addresses non-monetary factors in employment, from flexible schedules to tailored benefit packages and development opportunities. The Marriott Hotel City Center in downtown Denver set up an endowment for the University of Denver's Hotel Management Program for students studying hospitality-hotel management.

As part of Marriott's Pathways to Independence: A Training-of-Jobs program, disadvantaged individuals with development skills get training and support to develop skills for full-time employment and satisfying careers with Marriott and other hospitality industry employers.

Community Partnership

Marriott's extensive partnership with the communities in which it operates and the people it employs has been noticed by many. For example, the Hispanic College Fund named Marriott International the 1997 Corporate Partner of the Year for its financial donations; *Fortune* magazine rated Marriott International among the 50 best companies for Asians, blacks, and Hispanics; and *Working Mother* magazine rated Marriott International among the 100 best companies for working mothers, making it the only hospitality company to be so recognized. Also, *Business Week* and *Working Mother* magazines rated Marriott International among the top 20 family-friendly companies; *CIO* magazine picked Marriott International as one of the top companies to excel in the 21st century; and *Latina Style* magazine rated Marriott International among the top 50 companies for Latinos.

"Marriott's value proposition is genuine care, dependability, and a sense of community," says Marriott. "That's our proposition to associates, too. When they come to work, there's no telling what problems they face at home. They can come here and feel safe, secure, and welcome."

While Marriott International puts its heart in training employees and watching them advance, its soul is in the communities where it operates hotels. The Marriott Hotel City Center in Denver, for example, provided free catering services for the 2000 Martin Luther King Jr. Awards Banquet at the Denver Center for the Performing Arts.

Fairfield Inn by Marriott is a national sponsor of Habitat for Humanity International, dating to 1995. To date, Fairfield Inn has contributed volunteer labor and funds toward the completion of nearly 48 homes. At the corporate level, Fairfield Inn has committed to sponsoring at least two houses each year. Individual hotels also work with Habitat to provide funding and volunteer labor.

Marriott International has been involved with Children's Miracle Network (CMN) since the network's inception in 1982. Since 1984, the company has supported CMN's 170

At all Marriott hotels, highly trained employees make guests' stays welcoming and relaxing.

children's hospitals, including Children's Hospital in Denver, with nearly $11 million in contributions and donated services.

Since 1996, Marriott associates have increased the company's national involvement through their Marriott Pride program, which accounted for the lion's share of the company's $2 million donation. Working together, Courtyard; Fairfield; Residence Inn; Marriott Hotels, Resorts, and Suites; Sodexho Marriott Services; Host Marriott Services; and Host Marriott have embraced Marriott Pride and developed several successful fund-raising campaigns. Combined with corporate support from all three Marriott companies, Marriott presented Children's Miracle Network with $2.5 million on the organization's national broadcast in June.

Marriott attributes much of the company's thinking today to his parents, whom he describes as caring people who were also businesspeople. He often repeats their philosophy that "if they took care of the associates, the associates would take care of the guest."

As part of the Marriott way of doing business, every employee in every department

Marriott can provide catering and convention services for groups large and small.

of Marriott's full-service hotels participates in a 15-minute meeting daily, reviewing the company's basic principles. Included in the list of basic principles are items on practicing teamwork; using respect for each other, just as would be used for family and guests; having genuine care; and covering technical matters.

"We also give each associate an oppor-

tunity to raise his or her personal concerns," says Marriott. "Most important, we take the time to celebrate everyone's birthday and anniversaries. We call this the loyalty program because it builds loyalty among our associates and repeat business from our customers. The end result is that everyone feels he or she has a stake in making the hotel a success."

From the sophisticated downtown Marriott Hotel City Center to the newly renovated Renaissance Hotel across from the former Stapleton International Airport, Denver has been a strong market for the $17.7 billion company that operates some 2,000 hotels and resorts in 59 countries, including nearly 40 throughout Colorado.

Many Marriott hotels feature fine dining and entertainment in a relaxed atmosphere.

Radisson Stapleton Plaza

Located minutes east of downtown Denver and 20 minutes from Denver International Airport (DIA), Radisson Stapleton Plaza has stood the test of time, growing and evolving with the changes in the area. As occupancy rates plunged when nearby Stapleton International Airport closed in 1995, the hotel dusted itself off with a $12 million renovation, and today enjoys a flourishing business with occupancy rates as high as 90 percent. ● As changes to the 25-year-old hotel got under way, the Stapleton Development Corporation—the city's steward for redeveloping the 4,700-acre site of the former airport—kicked off plans to create a diverse urban neighborhood of homes, shops, offices, and parks, essentially creating a new community covering 7.5 square miles.

Renovation and Redevelopment

When DIA opened, our occupancy slid to 40 or 50 percent," says Dermot Connolly, Radisson managing director. "We had to sit and wait and be creative in bringing in a different kind of business. Then, Radisson came in and invested heavily in renovations, and we led the charge among Stapleton hotels."

According to Connolly, "There is no other metro area in the country that has this much developable land available. And we're sitting on the doorstep of this new community, which will serve as an alternative to downtown Denver as we're located between DIA and downtown. With all the infrastructure that comes with the project, such as improved roads, this is as good as it gets."

The ambitious Stapleton redevelopment, which will attract 30,000 residents and 35,000 workers by its completion in 2030, is just one of the reasons Minneapolis-based Radisson Hotels & Resorts Worldwide saw promise in its Stapleton property investment. Stapleton's central location ultimately will be enhanced by the development of a commuter rail line connecting downtown Denver with DIA. One of the four stops is expected to be located close to Stapleton and the nearby Radisson.

Since the Stapleton airport's closure,

United Airlines has invested $250 million to upgrade its Stapleton Flight Training Center into the most sophisticated facility of its kind in the world. Foreign airlines contract with United for pilot training, giving the Radisson a foreign flair, as international pilots stay there. Other flight-related businesses, including a pilot-training school, are housed in the hotel's office tower.

Appealing Amenities

The 300-room hotel underwent a complete renovation—from its tucked-away infrastructure and computer system to its decor highlighted by a striking, 11-story, indoor atrium. Guestrooms with views of the majestic Rocky Mountains and stunning downtown Denver also open onto the hotel's atrium.

"Every room was redone into a business-class room, including our luxury suites," says

Connolly. "All of our rooms are equipped for doing business with two-line speaker phones; dataport/high-speed Internet access; a large, 54-inch desk; and an ergonomic leather chair."

The Radisson's 24,000-square-foot, newly renovated conference center offers flexible meeting space with up to 26 meeting rooms that can accommodate diverse groups from five to 340 people. The complete Business Center offers a full range of mailing and secretarial services, while the 10,000-square-foot Fitness Center offers a heated outdoor pool, aerobics classes, racquetball courts, personal trainers, and an on-site massage therapist.

Radisson Stapleton Plaza has several restaurants, including Quebec's Bistro for full-service casual dining, Staples Deli, and Martini's Lounge, which includes pool tables and piano-bar entertainment. In addition, room service is available.

"We provide 24-hour shuttle service to

The Radisson Stapleton Plaza is located next to the Stapleton Office Center.

Business class guestrooms feature a view of downtown Denver and the Rocky Mountains (left).

The 11-story lobby features seven juniper trees (right).

and from DIA," says Connolly, adding that shuttles also run to the Cherry Creek shopping district and downtown. "We're still in a vibrant, lucrative market for hotels, even though the planes don't fly out of Stapleton any longer."

Genuine Hospitality

The new Radisson logo went up on Radisson Stapleton Plaza in April 2000, crowning the renovation and standing as a beacon across from the new

Stapleton community. The logo, produced in Oslo by advertising design agency Interaction Brand, was created by studying autographs of famous people, including Radisson's namesake, French explorer Pierre Esprit Radisson.

"There's a brush stroke under the Radisson name symbolizing the final brush stroke of Genuine Hospitality," says Connolly, pointing to the distinctive bold, green brush stroke. He says guests regularly write to thank employees such as James, a front desk clerk, who went above and beyond the call of duty to

locate a guest's lost luggage. "He was friendly, funny, and completely competent," a guest wrote corporate headquarters. Connolly takes it in stride, saying, "That's what we stand for, Genuine Hospitality."

Radisson operates in 53 countries, adding a record 55 new locations in 2000, and expanding for the first time into South Africa, Mauritius, Oman, Turkey, and Uruguay. In Europe, Radisson is represented by two of the world's most upscale hotel companies, Radisson SAS Hotels Worldwide and Radisson Edwardian Hotels (in London).

The hotel's many amenities include (clockwise from top left) the Arapahoe Ballroom; the Aztec Ballroom; Quebec's Bistro, led by Executive Chef Jason Raynes; and Martini's Lounge and Piano Bar.

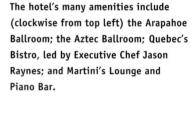

The complete Business Center is available around the clock (left).

The staff is always ready to greet each guest with Genuine Hospitality (right).

Durrant has a history of building Colorado. "With a professional story that dates back nearly 70 years, we have demonstrated our professional commitment with enthusiasm and innovation in a challenging business climate," says William A. Baker, managing director of Durrant's Rocky Mountain region. ● Durrant currently consists of 14 offices in nine states employing more than 350 people, and provides specialized architecture, engineering, and construction management services to clientele in the retail, criminal justice, education, and health care arenas in the United States and abroad.

Founded by Joe Durrant in Wisconsin in 1933, The Durrant Group, Inc., Durrant's parent company, has grown to become one of *Engineering News-Record*'s (ENR) top 250 firms in the United States. Durrant's Mountain Region, based in Denver, has offices in Colorado Springs, Austin, San Antonio, and St. Louis.

In Colorado, Durrant dates back to the 1950s to a firm called Flickinger & Associates. Through a collaborative effort with retail magnate Jordan Perlmutter, Flickinger & Associates put its stamp on such notable projects as Northglenn Mall, Southglenn Mall, and Southwest Plaza, and began a long relationship with signature retailer May Department Stores. In 1985, The Durrant Group acquired Flickinger & Associates to form Durrant Flickinger, later to be called Durrant.

Scott Halpin, AIA, the managing principal of Durrant's Denver office, remembers those formative years: "The mid- to late '80s was an era when development was at a standstill in Colorado and the bottom had fallen out of the Denver economy. We were fortunate enough to find our niche in retail and it has rewarded us ever since." Soon, other retail projects followed, including a new Foley's Department Store and the subsequent expansion of Lord & Taylor in the Cherry Creek Shopping Center. "Those premier stores were the beginning of a client relationship that has lasted nearly 20 years," says Halpin.

A Diverse Portfolio

Although Durrant's Colorado reputation was built on retail, the company's overall specialties go beyond the retail market to include adult correctional, juvenile, and law enforcement facilities; kindergarten-through-grade-12 and higher-education facilities; and recreation centers. In response to an increasing demand for justice facilities on a national level, Durrant has created a professional Justice Studio in Colorado. Locally, the company has worked on new projects that include the Colorado Springs Police Operations Center, Robert M. Isaac Municipal Courts, and Washington County Criminal Justice Center.

The same Durrant team has also excelled in privatized justice work in Texas, Georgia, Ohio, and Pennsylvania; a recent project is a $50 million adult correctional facility for the Federal Bureau of Prisons. Even with an excellent track record in retail and justice markets, Durrant understands the need to diversify its services and expand its expertise. "The

In response to an increasing demand for justice facilities on a national level, Durrant has created a professional Justice Studio in Colorado.

state of Colorado is growing, and will continue to require new schools, health care facilities, and recreation centers," says Halpin. "As an employee-owned company, we are dedicated to expanding our knowledge base and services to meet the changing needs of our clients."

While Durrant is primed for Colorado's growth, the company also gleans a sense of history through its rich past and strives to maintain Colorado's heritage through historic preservation projects, including working with the Colorado Historic Society. Durrant's historic preservation work is led by Robert Stegmueller, AIA, principal of Durrant. "We are fortunate to live in a place like Colorado where so much rich history has taken place," says Stegmueller. "We strive to leave this world better than we found it, and we do so through preservation and adaptive reuse. I like to define architecture as the design of a building to be used for many functions over a long life. We, as historic architects, are the caretakers of that building."

Durrant is honored to have worked on various historic preservation projects throughout Colorado, viewing those opportunities as a way of giving back to the community. Durrant has assisted the Colorado Historical Society in assessing the condition of 26 historic landmarks, including the Grant-Humphries Mansion in Denver, the Healy House in Leadville, the Barglow House in Trinidad, and Fort Garland.

A Future of Growth

With a hand in Colorado's past and an eye on Colorado's future, Durrant is moving into the new millennium as a architecture/engineering/construction management firm with a stable foundation built on experience, service, and knowledge-based growth. Recently, the company designed several signature department stores at Park Meadows Mall and Flatiron Crossing Mall, and is currently working with

Denver-based Ultimate Electronics and restaurant developer Tricon Global. "Maintaining ongoing client relationships is our way of growing and maintaining business," says Dennis Thompson, AIA, principal of Durrant. "We listen to our clients, anticipate new trends, and design facilities that meet the needs of a growing economy." From large department stores to small boutiques, Durrant goes the extra mile for its clients. "Because retailers are on such strict deadlines with solid opening dates, we can't just limit ourselves to traditional architecture," says Thompson. "We do whatever it takes to get the job done. Hands-on project management is the key to every project we undertake."

"Our vision is to provide superior service to all clients," says Baker. "These are exciting times for our profession and our state. Colorado has opened new doors for us in the realm of the built environment, and we are prepared to walk, even sprint, toward the future."

Durrant's Colorado reputation was built on retail, including such notable projects as the Foley's Department Store (formerly May D&F) in both Flatiron Crossing Mall in Broomfield and Southwest Plaza Mall in Littleton.

HenryGill Advertising

Nestled in a downtown Denver skyscraper with the Rocky Mountains as an inspiring backdrop, HenryGill Advertising is no ordinary hometown agency. The region's oldest independent advertising agency attracts national talent to the local market. People of that caliber are drawn by HenryGill's reputation for being a creative place to work on top brands, as well as to enjoy Colorado's quality of life. ● Under the parent company of Mphasis, Inc., HenryGill, along with sister company Clarus Public Relations, offers clients all aspects of brand development and building,

including strategic marketing, planning, and administration; creative development and multimedia production, including television, radio, print, and new media campaigns; direct mail; media/new media planning and buying; and public relations.

At HenryGill, regional products are grown into national brands, while already established national brands, such as Dairy Queen and Mercedes-Benz, are given a regional touch. The HenryGill team consistently demonstrates its ability to maintain brand integrity across all disciplines of advertising, get its clients noticed, and get results. That competence comes from one thing, experience.

"We have a very senior staff with national experience," says David Henry, president, who founded the agency in 1977. Their résumés read like a "Who's Who" list of advertising agencies with Fortune 500 clients.

Most drive-thru service is pretty typical.

Only with tellers like Steve,

ours is anything but.

Not everyone at Guaranty is as entertaining as Steve, but they all have their own little ways of making people feel welcome and well cared for. While the people at Guaranty take their business and yours seriously, that's not how they take themselves. Believe it or not, they even make banking sort of fun. Talk to the people at Guaranty. 303-286-9800. www.guarantybankonline.com. People you can bank on.

Guaranty Bank

Surviving and Thriving

With capitalized annual billings of $30 million, HenryGill has grown substantially since Henry first opened his agency's doors in a suite in Denver's Cherry Creek business district. Soon after, he rented an office to Walter Gill, who eventually joined him as a partner. Together, they grew the business, even emerging

successfully from Denver's oil bust years, a time in which many other agencies failed. In 1992, the firm moved downtown. Gill retired from the agency in 1994.

"We've seen a lot of independent agencies go out of business or merge with other agencies," says Henry, "but we're attracting and holding the right people and have good long-term client relationships, like Guaranty Bank and Trust Co., whose chairman has been a client for 10 years."

HenryGill has an impressive client list that includes Dairy Queen, Guaranty Bank, AT&T Media Services, Global Telescope Network, Westcore Funds, WholeTree.com, Mercedes-Benz of Littleton, High Speed Access, the University of Phoenix, and Qdoba Mexican Grill. And the list keeps growing.

With business moving at lightning speed, Henry sees no end, or even a slowdown, in sight. "Now we're involved in building brands on the Internet, too," he says. "Early on, we invested in automating, working with computers, e-mail and other technology, long before others had adapted."

People and Passion

The firm and its team of creative, dedicated employees believe in staying on top of trends in film, television, music, and Internet, gleaning what makes consumers tick. "I don't know of any industry that has as much influence on a population that will grow to 6.6 billion people by 2003 as the advertising industry," says Alan Koenke, senior vice president/creative director. Koenke

From its offices in downtown Denver, HenryGill Advertising, under the direction of its seasoned senior management team, has created highly successful multimedia campaigns for Dairy Queen and Guaranty Bank.

**The firm's impressive client list also
includes Wholetree.com, Qdoba Mexican
Grill, Mercedes-Benz of Littleton, Global
Telescope Network, and Westcore Funds.**

is part of a senior team that also includes
Terry Datz, vice president/media director;
Chris Rhodes, vice president/director of
operations; Jane Brody Zales, vice president/
associate creative director; and David Pair,
CPA/controller.

"HenryGill is a client-focused advertising
agency," says Henry. "The value of our
advertising is that it builds equity within
companies."

As a member of the Marketing and Advertising Global Network (MAGNET), HenryGill's
geographical reach goes way beyond Denver.

MAGNET is comprised of approximately 36
leading agencies across the United States that
essentially act as branch offices from coast to
coast, and 20 agencies within Europe, which
serve in a similar capacity across the globe.

Koenke explains the HenryGill philosophy:
"We believe that, in order to provoke a response, advertising must evoke an emotion.
We say, affect equals effect." And all of the
work that comes out of the agency lives up
to its creed.

However, emotion is not only a part of
its work, but a part of its days as well. It's

quite apparent that this close-knit group
enjoys its work, its clients, and each other.
Koenke adds, "there's never a dull moment,
every day is different than the last. Best of
all, we have fun."

It's said about advertising agencies that
you can often tell the quality of their work
by the noise level and the laughter. Peruse
the halls at HenryGill and there's no doubt
that this sentiment is true. The office is alive,
the jovial mood is contagious, and the walls
are decorated with award showcases that
are over-stuffed.

S. A. Miro, Inc.

Founded in 1980 by Sami A. Miro, S. A. Miro, Inc. has a reputation for excellence in engineering throughout Colorado and the United States. The staff of some 75 dedicated employees offers varied engineering services, including consulting, civil, structural, and architectural engineering, as well as management services. ● S. A. Miro, Inc. made its mark on Colorado in the early 1980s, and, today, continues its engineering tradition with marquee projects such as the Denver International Airport, Denver Central Library, and Ocean Journey, the aquarium that brings the sea to Colorado.

Success through Diversity

During the oil-driven building boom of the early 1980s, S. A. Miro, Inc. established its engineering credentials with such projects as the 10-story Cherry Creek National Bank in Denver, the 13-story Stanford Corporate Center in Dallas, and the 19-story Mountain Towers Office Building in the Denver suburb of Glendale. But with the oil market collapse in the late 1980s, Denver's economy slowed and many firms either folded or moved. S. A. Miro, Inc. chose to diversify to survive the downturn. The firm capitalized on the core technical strengths of its staff members to quickly move beyond the design of new building projects and into diverse fields. "It was a wild ride in the mid-80s," says Miro. "We knew we were going to have to diversify to stay in business."

The first opportunity to diversify came from the U.S. Air Force Academy (USAFA), located north of Colorado Springs. As the academy passed its 25-year anniversary, its civil engineering staff had a huge task ahead—to modernize the infrastructure of the 3,000-acre facility. S. A. Miro, Inc. developed a 15-year plan for repair and replacement of the base roadways and, in the process, established a solid relationship with the USAFA staff that continues today.

Next came the design and construction of Denver International Airport (DIA), which represented the reawakening of the Colorado economy and new opportunity for S. A. Miro, Inc. From its signature tent roof to the highly efficient layout of the 54-square-mile airfield and access roadways, DIA was conceived to serve the needs of 21st-century travelers.

S. A. Miro, Inc. played a key role in designing many of the airport's major facilities, including the terminal. The firm's engineers designed the terminal floor structure to tie into the base of the tent roof. Working in close coordination with the tent designer, the firm's staff designed the anchors that secure the tent's cables to the structure. Included within the terminal is the structural envelope of the automated guideway transportation system's train network, which carries passengers underground to outlying concourses.

S. A. Miro, Inc.'s civil engineers were also part of a joint venture that designed Runway 17 Left/35 Right, one of five major elements of the airfield. "DIA put us on the map," says Miro. "That helped us attract other jobs and bring engineering students from across the nation to the firm."

Today, S. A. Miro, Inc. continues to support the development of Denver's gateway to the world through the firm's role in the DIA Business Partnership. The cooperative venture teams private corporations and public entities—including the Colorado cities of Aurora, Brighton, Commerce City, and Denver, and the E-470 Highway Authority—to promote economic development in the area influenced by DIA. Miro himself chaired the partnership's international committee in 1998-1999, playing a key role in the joint mission to London, which included the DIA Business Partnership, Denver Mayor Wellington Webb, and Colorado Governor Bill Owens. Miro's service

S. A. Miro, Inc. has served as engineering consultant to the United States Air Force Academy since 1986 (top). Among the firm's major structural engineering projects are the Denver Central Library (bottom left) and Colorado's Ocean Journey Aquarium (bottom right).

will continue as he assumes the chairmanship of the partnership in 2001.

Dedicated to the Denver Community

The company's devotion to civic pride continued into 1991 when Denver voters approved a $60 million project to renovate the Denver Central Library and construct a 230,000-square-foot addition, tripling the library's square footage. S. A. Miro, Inc. served as structural and civil engineers for both the addition and the renovation projects, working with Michael Graves and Klipp, Colussy, Jenks, Dubois Architects. The S. A. Miro, Inc. staff took on significant technical challenges posed by a combination of heavy floor loading, complex geometry, and a wide variety of systems and materials.

After completion of the library, S. A. Miro, Inc. began work on a series of major office building projects that continues today, including headquarters buildings for TCI, American Family Insurance, and First Data Corporation. Over the past five years, the Miro team has engineered more than 3 million square feet of corporate office space.

Colorado's Ocean Journey, an engineering feat that brings the sea to life for Colo-

radans, began as the dream of Bill and Judy Fleming, and was funded entirely through private donations. The aquarium's design presented enormous technical challenges, which S. A. Miro, Inc. readily met. To ensure efficient use of the site, mechanical and life-support systems were placed directly below the exhibits. As a result, the floor structure had to carry the tremendous weight of the display tanks, lifelike canyons, and pedestrian gathering places. Adding to the complexity of the structure was the construction of a circular atrium, which provides an inviting entry and rendezvous area, as well as an open display for the aquarium's river otters.

S. A. Miro, Inc. enters the 21st century continuing its service to the Front Range, where staff members have deep roots, and supporting the cultural, religious, and service organizations of the area. As Colorado's economy continues to boom, the firm recruits top candidates from graduate schools and firms throughout the Midwest and the eastern seaboard.

As S. A. Miro, Inc.'s structural staff continues to work on major building projects, the company's civil team continues its tradition of major campus infrastructure support, design-

ing the utility infrastructure at the former Fitzsimmons Army Medical Center, which will be the new home to the University of Colorado Health Sciences Center. Working with Integrated Planning and Engineering, the civil team is producing documents for the science center's new utility systems. "In keeping with our plan to offer diverse services, we continue to be at the forefront of firms that innovate, challenge existing methods and conceptions, and seek to apply our expertise in new areas," says Miro.

S. A. Miro, Inc. played a key role in the design of Denver International Airport, including the Landside Terminal (top); at the Air Force Academy, the firm devised a unique load-enhancement method for a dormitory floor (bottom left). The firm also designed the structural system of Ocean Journey (bottom right).

TRW Inc.

From a modest start about 20 years ago, Data Systems Operations (DSO) of TRW Inc. has grown into one of the Denver area's leading software developers and systems operators for the federal government, providing services for nationally important systems in addition to data management and tech support. ● While most of what DSO does is classified, the operation has fulfilled its corporate promise by becoming one of the nation's largest contractors to the U.S. Department of the Interior's Bureau of Land Management (BLM). This relationship has been growing since 1994, but DSO has no time to rest on its laurels.

Growing Services

DSO provides the BLM with technical support services, covering everything from a help desk to participation in field surveys. The company also provides development and management for the BLM's geographic information systems and Landsat data, system administration, and computer network software integration.

For example, when President Bill Clinton called upon the BLM to provide a map of the nation's newest national monument to display at the press conference announcing the monument's formation, DSO quickly produced this map. DSO provides cost-effective data management and support for a wide variety of BLM programs, and hopes to broaden that support to more Interior Department agencies.

At Home in the Mile High City

Denver is a natural place for DSO— which got its start in the suburb of Aurora with one person in 1980— because the Mile High City has the largest population of nonmilitary federal workers outside of Washington, D.C. Located near Buckley Air Force Base, as well as at the Denver Federal Center, the company is now housed in five buildings. After TRW won an important data processing contract from the government in 1982, more contracts followed, and the size and importance of the Denver operation blossomed. By 1990, the company had evolved from operating data systems into an organization that also specializes in the development and integration of leading-edge computer systems for the government.

TRW conducts much of its software development work at this facility in Aurora, a Denver suburb.

Data Systems Operations (DSO) of TRW Inc. Director Dr. Robert Lindeman and Senior Research Scientist Ardis Scott discuss the hardware architecture supporting a current computer-learning research project. DSO is active in researching self-evolving computing environments based on Beowulf clusters and agent technology.

Since that time, DSO has become an important component of TRW's aerospace and information systems structure, employing almost 900 people in the Denver area.

DSO's employees are actively involved in supporting their community through programs such as home construction for Habitat for Humanity, providing Christmas gifts to needy families through the Comitis Crisis Center, volunteering in local schools, and teaching at the university level. DSO also serves the community through a group called the Employee Charitable Organization, which channels employee charitable contributions to a wide variety of local nonprofit organizations.

Looking to Expand

While Department of Defense applications are DSO's bread and butter, DSO Director Robert Lindeman is looking to expand the nondefense side of the corporation. As government agencies are asked to do more work with less money, they will be looking for ways to make their personnel more productive, while outsourcing technical work to businesses that can perform for the best value. That's where DSO steps in.

"We see a market for expanding our technical services to new civil federal agencies," says Lindeman. However, he is unwilling to limit that expansion simply to federal agencies. Lindeman is looking into state and local government applications for DSO, and he can point to an impressive measure of success in the company's goals.

Revenues from DSO have increased 450 percent in the last 10 years. Success, however, isn't just measured in dollars. In fact, all of DSO's respondents to the last customer satisfaction survey, taken late in 1999, said they were very satisfied with the overall value of the work done by DSO.

ISO Registered and SEI Assessed

In order to show customers that DSO has the quality standards and procedures in place to be a top performer, the company was audited and has been registered by the British Standards Institute as an ISO 9001-registered site. In addition, DSO was recently assessed as compliant with the Software Engineering Institute's (SEI) Capability Maturity Model at Level 3.

From its beginnings in 1901 as the Cleveland Cap Screw Company, TRW has seen tremendous growth. With offices now in 35 countries, the company has become an international supplier of air bags and safety systems from the automotive groups, as well as satellite and defense systems from the aerospace groups.

Along the way, TRW helped land the first men on the moon. Pioneer 10, also a TRW project, was the first man-made object to leave the solar system. On Earth, though, TRW leaves much of the pioneering of the information technology processing in the capable hands of Data Systems Operations.

Clockwise from top:
This image was created by draping a multi-spectral satellite image over a digital terrain model. TRW uses data sets like these in its support to BLM land managers.

In the new millennium, satellite communications are a critical element in TRW's multifaceted business line.

TRW uses its people and resources to assist the community in a variety of ways. For example, the company has sent teams of about 15 people to help Habitat for Humanity build homes for low-income residents.

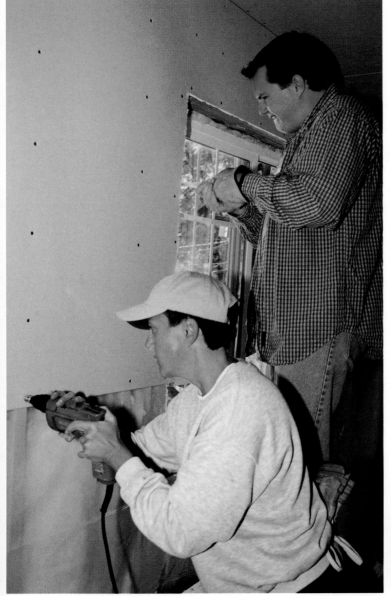

1981-1994

1987	Colorado Office of Economic Development and International Trade
1987	Pacific Western Technologies, Ltd.
1988	CIBER Inc.
1989	Univision 50/KCEC-TV
1991	PEAK Resources Inc.
1991	ProLogis
1992	Freeman Group Public Relations
1993	Insurance Design & Placement, Inc.
1993	KeyBank/McDonald Investments Inc.

Colorado Office of Economic Development and International Trade

Colorado's history of booms and busts was never more apparent than when the oil boom of the 1970s turned into the economic bust of the 1980s. In 1987, the Colorado General Assembly responded by consolidating the state's major economic development and international trade programs into the Governor's Office. These programs, now part of the Colorado Office of Economic Development and International Trade, are charged with fostering a positive business climate that encourages quality economic development throughout the state of Colorado. ● Today, the state's picture is a positive one, with many well-respected economic surveys consistently ranking Colorado among the top economies in the United States. The 1999 *State New Economy Index*, produced by the Progressive Policy Institute, rated Colorado third in the nation for states most advanced in emerging toward a new economy.

Sweeping Economic Rankings

The Corporation for Enterprise Development, which rates the competitiveness of all 50 states, awarded Colorado its prestigious straight A's for the seventh year in a row. Supporting economic indicators rank Colorado second in technology companies as a percentage of all firms. Colorado also boasts the highest percentage of adults who hold college degrees. The state enjoys high marks in economic diversity and long-term job growth. Colorado also places second in gross state product (GSP) growth, and is projected to remain in the top five states through 2005.

The high marks Colorado has earned for economic performance complement its quality of life. In fact, Morgan Quitno Publishing Company's *State Rankings 2000* awarded Colorado the number three spot in its Most Livable State Index. The state's climate offers 300 days of sunshine a year, and with 43 state and national parks, Colorado is famous for its natural beauty. This may explain why Colorado is one of the country's premier travel and tourism destinations.

"Colorado has an abundance of natural and human resources," says Bill Owens, governor of Colorado. "Our entrepreneurial spirit and quality of life consistently place us among the top states in the country for new business start-ups. And on a per capita basis, we currently rank second in the nation for new companies."

Supporting Economic Development

The Office of Economic Development and International Trade offers financial and technical assistance for eco-nomic development efforts. Whether an entrepreneur is just starting a business, or an established company wants to go international, the state is committed to serve.

Bob Lee, director of the Colorado Office of Economic Development and International Trade, explains that because many Colorado communities are competing for new businesses with similar communities across the country, the state office will remain flexible in order to support local development efforts. "In keeping with a statewide approach, our economic development team works with all Colorado communities and a variety of companies," says Lee. "A win-win proposition is

MONTY NUSS PHOTOGRAPHY

DAVID CORNWELL

LARRY PIERCE/STEAMBOAT SKI & RESORT CORPORATION

Clockwise from top left:
Governor Bill Owens was sworn in as Colorado's 40th governor on January 12, 1999, becoming the first Republican to be elected governor since 1971.

Bob Lee, director for the Office of Economic Development and International Trade, will parlay his successful private sector experience in real estate toward economic development efforts in Colorado.

Steamboat is nationally ranked as one of the top resorts for families.

our goal, with good corporate citizens providing high-quality jobs to Coloradans. This philosophy will foster a superior business climate that allows companies, both new and existing, to grow and prosper in Colorado."

Owens believes that state economic development efforts should enhance local efforts. "Because of Colorado's wonderful diversity, economic development means something different to each community," says Owens. "Ultimately, economic development decisions are determined locally. While a company may decide to relocate or expand into Colorado, it will establish itself in the community that best matches its specific labor, transportation, and infrastructure needs."

Encouraging Economic Diversity

The quality of life and cluster of technology-based businesses make Colorado attractive to high-tech companies," says Lee. "In fact, we enjoy the highest concentration of high-tech workers in the country. With much of this activity occurring along the Front Range–from Fort Collins to Pueblo–we'd like to see a more statewide dispersion of economic activity, and are now investing in infrastructures to encourage this."

Along with an increased focus on the rural areas of Colorado, Owens supports international trade and has led missions to promote Colorado's reach into the global marketplace. With Colorado companies last year exporting $6.4 billion in manufactured goods and agricultural products, it's obvious the world has taken notice. Colorado currently ships about 37 percent of its exports to Europe, 38 percent to Asia, and 23 percent to Canada and Latin America combined.

"I see a bright future for international trade in Colorado," says Lee. "For many years, our dominant exports have been relatively high-value items, as well as agricultural products. Most of the manufactured products fall into categories such as computer and electronic equipment, medical products and scientific instruments, or other sorts of industrial and commercial equipment. As the worldwide need for food increases and trade restrictions are lowered, agricultural items should also see continued and growing demand."

Not since the silver and gold rush days of the 1880s has Colorado's outlook been brighter. This time, however, the economy, from the Eastern Plains to the Western Slope, is both diversified and prosperous.

Clockwise from top:
Owens and former British Prime Minister Margaret Thatcher discuss international affairs during a U.K. Trade Mission in July 1999.

The Office of Economic Development and International Trade, located in Colorado's World Trade Center, fosters a positive business climate by assisting local and regional economic development activities throughout the state.

Horseback riding in Steamboat Springs demonstrates why Colorado is one of the country's year-round premier travel and tourism destinations.

Pacific Western Technologies, Ltd.

Pacific Western Technologies, Ltd. (PWT), one of the fastest-growing small businesses in Colorado, offers a variety of technical consulting services, including information management, program management and control, and environmental consulting. Dr. Tai-Dan Hsu, president, is the visionary of the company, while his business partner and wife, Ding-Wen Hsu, chief operating officer, makes sure the vision becomes a reality. ● "I like to sit around and dream about the future," says Tai-Dan Hsu, who has a Ph.D. in hydrology from the University of Iowa. "We share our dreams and visions with our employees. We treat them as family. That's why we are able to generate a lot of enthusiasm and excitement among our employees."

Growing into Prominence

But growing the business into such prominence—recognized in 1995, 1997, and 2000 with a U.S. Small Business Administration (SBA) Administrators Award of Excellence—was not always easy. "We used up all of our savings, borrowed from our life insurance policy, mortgaged our house, and were $100,000 in debt at the end of 1991," recalls Hsu. "My wife was working for a software development company and got laid off. It was a difficult time, especially when the phone didn't ring."

Forging ahead, the company founders applied for certification under the SBA's 8(a) Contracting and Business Development Program, which levels the playing field for minority- and women-owned small businesses with large corporations seeking government procurement contracts. In 1992, Recom Technologies in San Jose asked PWT to team with it and compete on a five-year, $7.5 million contract offered by the Western Area Power Administration, a branch of the U.S. Department of Energy operations in Denver. "I had never written such a large proposal before, but we won, and it was the contract that got us started on a solid foundation," says Hsu.

In 1994, after earning her MBA from the University of Colorado at Denver, Ding-Wen Hsu joined PWT full time as chief operating officer. "In working together, we find our strengths and weaknesses and build on them," she says. "He's more focused on the long term and is constantly dreaming up things, while my personality is more on the analytical side, overseeing the daily details."

Today, PWT has grown to employ more than 180 people in Lakewood, Colorado; Oak Ridge, Tennessee; San Antonio, Texas; and Albuquerque, New Mexico. In addition, the company has a subsidiary, Waste Abatement Technology, located in Marietta.

Even with this success, PWT is not resting on its laurels. Seldom, admits Tai-Dan Hsu, is he not thinking three to five years down the road, toward the next acquisition or series of contracts that he expects will grow the company to revenues of $50 million. Eventually, he sees an initial public offering in PWT's future. For his vision and performance, the SBA in 1998 named Hsu the National Minority Business Person of the Year, while in 1998, Ernst & Young singled out PWT as one of the best entrepreneurial companies of the year.

A More Efficient World through the Use of Technologies

PWT's mission statement says a lot about the company and what the Hsus stand for: "Pacific Western Technologies contributes to the success of our clients by providing high quality, responsive, technical and management services while maintaining the highest ethical environment for our employees and our business partners."

Adjusting to market conditions, PWT has shifted its focus from hard-core engineering services to the areas of information management, program management and control, and environmental consulting. While PWT grew about 15 percent in 1999, the company has grown at an average rate of 40 percent since 1992. "Our goals are to see what our customers' needs are, then diversify to meet those needs," says Hsu, who, as founder of the Rocky Mountain Chinese Chamber of Commerce and board member of the Asian Chamber in Denver, is no stranger to innovation. "No matter how difficult the

Clockwise from top:
Pacific Western Technologies, Ltd. (PWT) is headquartered in Lakewood, Colorado.

PWT is working with the Department of Energy's Office of Civilian Radioactive Waste Management to investigate the suitability of a site in southern Nye County, Nevada, as the repository for spent nuclear fuel and high-level radioactive waste.

PWT's network administration staff designs, manages, and maintains the U.S. Geological Survey's Yucca Mountain Project Branch Microsoft NT server network.

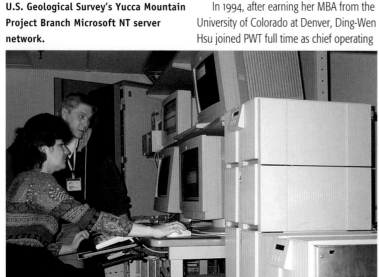

situation I run into, I always think very positively."

According to Hsu, federal budget cuts, which have forced many government agencies and large corporations to downsize or outsource numerous facility management operations, have been a boon to small businesses like PWT. The company created an infrastructure that efficiently handles government and corporate outsourcing activities such as computer facility operation, records management, quality assurance, and administrative and facility management. As a result, PWT has been called in to work on several program management projects for the federal government, including the Yucca Mountain Project, under U.S. Geological Survey administration, and the U.S. Department of Energy's Oak Ridge National Laboratory project.

Unflagging optimism and not being afraid to think big are Hsu's ingredients for success. With focused effort and marketing strategies, he believes PWT will enjoy a bigger share of the technical services market. Hsu's next goal is to take PWT public and build a $100 million corporation by 2005.

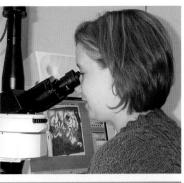

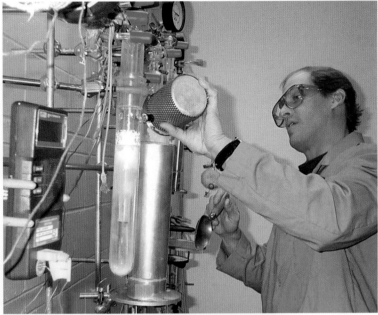

Clockwise from top right:
A PWT geologist examines fluid inclusions in a rock thin-section under the microscope.

A PWT chemist performs an analysis of tritium in a volcanic rock pore-water sample.

This aerial photograph of Hoover Dam was taken by PWT's Mapping Division.

The PWT staff downloads hydrologic data in the Exploratory Studies Facility at the Yucca Mountain, Nevada, test site.

CIBER Inc. was founded in 1974 in Detroit to serve the information technology (IT) needs of the giant auto industry. By 1988, the company had made its way onto the Colorado landscape, and today is an industry leader in providing E-business solutions for the Global 2000, the middle market, new scaling companies, and all levels of government. ● Backed by a 27-year history and a 90 percent client-renewal rate, CIBER has earned a deserved reputation as a trusted technology leader, enabling businesses to be agile, scalable, and connected. The company collaborates with customers to consistently and cost-effectively

plan, execute, and deliver high-quality services and results. CIBER utilizes seasoned professional consultants to build long-term, trusted relationships, and brings a high level of energy, integrity, experience, and value to client work.

The company has grown exponentially since its founding by three partners, including Bob Stevenson, who in 1978 became full owner of the company and today remains chairman of CIBER's board of directors. CIBER's consolidated revenues have skyrocketed from $48 million in 1994 to about $700 million in 1999.

"Our growth is a testament to being in a great industry, our top-notch employees, and our commitment to excellence, as well as CIBER's evolving business model," says Mac Slingerlend, CIBER president and chief executive officer, who joined the company in 1989.

Mac Slingerlend, CIBER Inc.'s president and chief executive officer, has been with CIBER since 1989.

Helping Businesses Conduct E-Business

Headquartered in Greenwood Village, Colorado, since 1988, CIBER and its subsidiaries employ some 5,500 people in 50 offices across the United States, Canada, and Europe. CIBER's IT consulting services focus on several areas, including strategic IT and management consulting, E-business solutions, enterprise software solutions, custom IT solutions, systems and network integration, and enterprise outsourcing.

"Both the Internet and enabling technologies have changed the way the world does business—whether it's buying or selling products, or the way customers and companies relate," says Slingerlend. "It is changing the way society interacts and transforming the business world daily."

CIBER is there to help companies develop the Internet-technology foundation they need to conduct E-business capable of serving customers 24 hours a day. Recently CIBER introduced the innovative .com in-a-box™, with which the company's IT staff quickly designs and conveniently maintains a client's Internet needs.

CIBER has also developed strong partnerships with superior technology vendors, allowing CIBER to remain objective while working with clients to determine the most appropriate hardware, software, and services to meet their business requirements.

CIBER subsidiaries include DigiTerra, Inc. in Englewood, which provides end-to-end Internet solutions to middle market companies, and Neovation, Inc. in Greenwood Village, a global digital strategy agency. Enspherics, Inc. in Englewood joined CIBER in November 2000; its focus is high-threat computer security environments. In addition, in 2000 CIBER entered into a joint venture with several companies, including Denver-based Verio, Inc., the world's largest Web-hosting company, to create Agilera, Inc., a leading application service provider (ASP).

CIBER insiders aren't the only ones to recognize the public company's astounding performance and innovation. *Forbes* magazine ranked CIBER among the nation's best small companies from 1994 through 1997. *Fortune* named CIBER one of the top 100 fastest-growing companies in 1998 and 1999, and *ColoradoBiz* magazine awarded CIBER its 1999 Company of the Year Award in the information technology category. *Smart Partner* named CIBER to its list of smart companies in 1999 and 2000.

At the time he accepted the *ColoradoBiz* honor, Slingerlend expressed his pride at being headquartered in Colorado: "We are very proud to be an ambassador for our state."

CIBER area directors review cross-selling opportunities in their local markets.

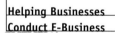
▲ WILLIAM SWARTZ PHOTOGRAPHY

Sitting in a tiny office in Lakewood in 1991, Vince DeRose and a couple of associates with an entrepreneurial spirit decided they would start a business providing high-tech solutions to corporate America. They put their money together and hung their shingle; PEAK Resources Inc., a computer hardware reseller, was open for business. ● PEAK is today located in a suite of offices in Denver. The company employs 40 people and is designated an IBM Premier Business Partner, one of only 200 businesses in the world to earn the prestigious status. PEAK has evolved into

one of the top high-tech solution providers in the Rocky Mountain region, and, even more impressive, is the number one printer reseller in the United States for IBM Printing Systems Division.

"We've grown 30 percent each year since 1995," says DeRose, PEAK president. "We had some lean years early on, but we turned the corner in 1996. Many things started coming together once we got the partnership with IBM in 1995. We worked hard for nine months to get that. It has always been our objective to establish and maintain relationships with large manufacturers, such as IBM. With the boom in the high-tech industry, we just keep growing." Joining DeRose on the PEAK management team are partners Haydn Hirstein, vice president of sales; Tom Brinegar, chief financial officer; and John Simonton, assistant vice president.

Strategic Partnerships

Many have taken notice of PEAK's performance. *Colorado Biz* magazine ranked the company 132nd of the top 250 companies in Colorado. And Illinois-based Lakeview Technology, the nation's number one provider of availability management software, tapped PEAK to be its only authorized reseller in the region. Oracle also signed an exclusive joint marketing agreement with PEAK.

"The Oracle and IBM agreements give PEAK exclusive marketing rights in Colorado, Wyoming, and New Mexico," says DeRose, explaining that while PEAK does do some national business, the company concentrates on the Rocky Mountain region.

Other leaders in the manufacture of information systems and software who partner with PEAK include Network Appliance,

AVNET Computer Marketing, Cisco Systems, Nortel Networks, and Paradyne.

"By combining our resources with these relationships, we are able to help medium and large businesses build and support the infrastructure for their entire information systems and solutions," says DeRose. "Not only do we provide hardware, but we also have a staff of highly qualified people to provide service as well."

Besides providing hardware and the skills required to operate systems, PEAK also offers project-based and custom services—everything from general systems administration to highly complex programs to meet customer needs. "Our goal is to become the premier advanced-technology solution provider for medium and large businesses in the Rocky Mountain region," says DeRose.

The **PEAK Resources Inc.** management team includes (from left) Vince DeRose, president; Haydn Hirstein, vice president of sales; John Simonton, assistant vice president; and Tom Brinegar, chief financial officer.

Univision 50/KCEC-TV is Denver's primary source for Spanish-language programming and a leading voice for the fastest-growing segment of Colorado's booming population—the Hispanic community. Broadcasting since 1989 as a Univision Television Network affiliate, KCEC-TV is a recognized leader for more than 500,000 Hispanics across Colorado through its local news and sports programming, as well as its emphasis on community involvement. Its sister station, Univision 27/KGHB-TV in Colorado Springs, enjoys a strong community standing in the southern Colorado market, including Pueblo.

In little more than a decade after its founding, KCEC-TV today operates from a 12,000-square-foot office and studio complex near downtown Denver, doubling its original production space. State-of-the-art facilities enable the staff of some 30 people to broadcast a new kind of excellence in television. From its early-morning network talk, news, and entertainment show, to game shows, variety shows, dramas, and local news and sports broadcasts, KCEC-TV is a full-time Spanish-language station, 24-hours a day, seven days a week.

"We broadcast a full range of Spanish-language programming produced in the United States and throughout the Spanish-speaking world," says Yrma Rico, general manager of KCEC-TV. "In 1995, we added local news and sports broadcasts, which really made us a voice for the Spanish-speaking Colorado community."

Tapping a Niche Market

The Hispanic market is the fastest-growing market segment in Colorado," says Rico. "Along with the growth of the Hispanic population, our television station is also experiencing phenomenal growth. We've seen our advertising sales grow 27 to 33 percent every year for the past decade." There appears to be no end in sight, with sales in 2000 expected to outpace previous growth.

With median Hispanic household incomes now approaching $44,000, according to Univision data, and a local Hispanic buying power of $6.5 billion, advertisers are looking to the untapped market to grow sales, and are turning to stations such as KCEC-TV to get their message out to the right constituency.

The Univision 50/KCEC-TV local news team includes (from left) Luis Canela, Adriana Rodriguez, Sara Suarez, and Rodolfo Cardenas.

"Once an advertiser tests the station, they know it works," says Rico. "Their message is targeted to a very specific Hispanic audience, and they come to realize the Hispanic market is a viable market. Our viewers are in the growing mode, in the purchasing mode—buying their homes and furniture—and they are strong consumers."

An Extensive Reach

Entravision Communications in Santa Monica owns KCEC-TV. The Hispanic media giant is the only Hispanic group in the nation to own television and radio stations, outdoor media, and a major Latino market newspaper. Following acquisitions in May 2000, the multimedia company now owns 31 television stations, including 17 Univision affiliates; 63 radio stations; New York's *El Diario/La Prensa*; and 10,000 Hispanic-oriented billboards. Entravision financed its acquisitions through a $750 million initial public offering on the New York Stock Exchange.

KCEC-TV considers its affiliation with Univision a marquee value in Hispanic broadcasting. In its 30-year history, Univision—the largest and most-watched Spanish language network in the United States—has become the main source of news, information, and entertainment for nearly 30 million Hispanics.

Univision's reach is extensive: about 92 percent of all U.S. Hispanic households can view the network through its 42 broadcast affiliates and estimated 831 cable affiliates. Univision has about an 80 percent share of the U.S. Spanish-language network television audience.

Contributing to the Community

We're at the heart of the Hispanic community," says Rico. "We also get involved in the community by sponsoring or participating in community events."

Almost monthly, KCEC-TV is involved in or orchestrates a community event. In January, Hispanic Coloradans who have made a difference in their communities are invited to the Hispanic Annual Salute Banquet. Local and national celebrities cohost the event, which presents awards to winners.

In conjunction with the Denver Public Schools, KCEC-TV each month nominates students from all grade levels for Bilingual Student of the Month recognition. The honor comes with the broadcast of a three-minute story on each student, highlighting his or her achievements.

Other events in which KCEC-TV plays a role include the National Hispanic Scholarship Fund Ski Fiesta in February, Cinco de Miles

5K Run/Walk in May, KCEC/Elitch Gardens Summer Fiesta in June, Latin Music and Arts Festival in July, Chile Festival in August, Mexican Independence Day Festival in September, and a clothing and toy drive in December. KCEC-TV also participates in long-standing Colorado events such as the National Western Stock Show's Mexican Rodeo Extravaganzas, the Parade of Lights winter celebration through downtown, and the Cherry Creek Arts Festival, the nation's third-largest outdoor arts festival.

"We believe strongly in community involvement and being a leader in supporting local events," says Rico. "As a leading business in the Hispanic community, we believe it is our corporate responsibility to take an active role in community events, or create events that are meaningful to our viewers—whether awarding scholarships or having fun at a Cinco de Mayo festival."

Focused on balancing programming excellence and community involvement, Univision 50/KCEC-TV not only occupies a niche in the television market, but also provides an invaluable service to an important part of Colorado's population. Consumer and market trends promise even greater possibilities for this unique organization to thrive in coming years.

Yrma Rico is general manager of KCEC-TV.

From an industrial park in Aurora, Colorado, ProLogis is revolutionizing the distribution facility business around the globe and is becoming a key player in the world of E-commerce. Founded in 1991, the company puts customers first and capital focus second in providing a complete distribution facility for companies expanding or reconfiguring their distribution requirements. ● "We pioneered the customer-driven approach to providing integrated distribution services and solutions on a global scale," says John W. Seiple, managing director and chief operating officer for ProLogis' North American Real Estate operations. "When we founded the company, we launched what has become the world's largest global distribution facility network. Our idea was to treat our clients like customers, not like tenants."

The customer-driven formula clearly is working, as ProLogis has more than 188 million square feet under development or operation in more than 1,600 facilities in some 94 U.S. and international markets. Annual revenue growth has been as phenomenal as square footage under contract, soaring from $1.6 million in 1992 to $345 million in 1998. Since an initial public offering in 1994, shareholders have averaged a 27.5 percent annualized return.

ProLogis targets the world's top 1,000 users of distribution space and provides facilities solutions to such industrial giants as Nestlé, Whirlpool, and Kodak. The company's multi-market customers include FedEx; Konica; Public Storage; Procter & Gamble; Sears, Roebuck & Co.; and United Parcel Service. To date, some 430 of ProLogis' Global 1,000 have signed on as customers, representing more than 40 percent of ProLogis' operating portfolio. In all, ProLogis has approximately 11,000 customers.

Thinking Globally

We think globally in everything we do, and that's why we have grown so rapidly," says Seiple. "With the emergence of the European Union, our research indicated there would be increased commerce, and ProLogis customers would need modern, high-volume distribution facilities in Europe."

ProLogis got its European expansion off the ground in 1997 by acquiring a facility in the port of Rotterdam, the largest port in the world. ProLogis then strategically expanded into seven other countries, including France, Germany, and the United Kingdom, where ProLogis signed a contract with Amazon.co.uk, a unit of Amazon.com Inc., for 728,000 square feet outside London.

"With E-commerce, companies are moving their inventories very, very quickly—much too rapidly, in fact, for them to get their distribution

ProLogis has more than 1,600 facilities either under development or in operation worldwide, including the Warsaw Industrial Center in Poland (top) and Hampton Central Distribution #2 in Maryland (bottom right).

John W. Seiple serves as North American managing director/chief operations officer of ProLogis (bottom left).

network set up," Seiple says. "That's where we come in—setting up that distribution network for them." ProLogis research from Forrester Research in Cambridge, Massachusetts, indicates that E-commerce is expected to grow to $105 billion by 2003, up from $7 billion in 1999.

"We've targeted accounts and allocated personnel to focus on E-commerce, and we believe that, by 2003, demand for additional distribution space could be 60 million to 100 million square feet in the United States alone," says Seiple.

An Extensive Roster of Quality Services

The ProLogis Operating System™ gives companies a competitive advantage by giving them access to ProLogis professionals who provide expertise in logistics, global capabilities, and financial strength—all with a single telephone call. The global services group, for example, includes 11 profes-

sionals who stay on top of the space requirements of a country's largest distribution users, while a 44-member global development group oversees delivery of new products.

In addition to leasing inventories, ProLogis builds custom facilities through its Corporate Distribution Facilities Development Group. A ProLogis team works with customers to tailor facilities to their needs, or help configure or streamline customers' supply chain procedures. The company also provides refrigerated distribution facilities in Europe and the United States through the world's largest global refrigerated distribution network.

To further expand its services, ProLogis acquired Meridian Industrial Trust Inc., a San Francisco-based industrial real estate investment trust, in early 1999. Meridian strengthens ProLogis' lead as a global supplier of distribution facilities and services, and gives ProLogis a strong presence in Los Angeles, Dallas, and Chicago, three of the biggest logistics markets in the United States. The

$1.5 billion merger added 68 customers to the ProLogis Global 1,000 database, and includes such marquee customers as the Ford Motor Co., IBM, Dow Electronics, Kraft Foods, Marriott International, Staples, and RJR Nabisco.

ProLogis also provides logistics consulting services through an affiliation with IN-SIGHT Management Support Services, the world leader in optimization-based logistics software. INSIGHT customers annually save 10 to 15 percent on logistics, optimizing their chain networks and distribution processes.

"From the beginning, we have always been a very research-oriented company, and have acted based on what our research indicated," Seiple says. "We've done a good job of creating a team, getting everyone on the same page, and understanding our mission and strategy. We have great people here, people who very much believe in our customer-service focus, and that's what sets us apart. We continue to build a world-class brand for world-class solutions."

Some of ProLogis' clients include (clockwise from top left) PDX, Caterpillar, FedEx, and Konica USA.

In 1955, Gerald Freeman founded Gerald Freeman, Inc., a New York/New Jersey public relations firm. Over the next several decades, Freeman and his wife, Sharon, together with key employees, developed the agency into one of the most widely recognized and esteemed public relations firms in the New York area. ● Almost half a century later, the setting has changed, along with most of the faces. But this husband-and-wife team is still going strong, and the name Freeman is still synonymous with the most knowledgeable, aggressive, and effective public relations counsel available.

A Home in Colorado

The firm's Colorado incarnation as Freeman Group Public Relations stems from the mid-1980s, when the Freemans moved to the Denver area, intending to retire. They soon became involved in regional politics, helping to win upset victories in a number of local campaigns. A full-fledged return to the field inevitably followed, and in 1992, the Freemans officially opened Freeman Group Public Relations in Colorado.

Today, with the addition of partner James Wall, Freeman Group Public Relations is a major presence in the state's business and political communities. According to the *Denver Business Journal*, the Denver office of Freeman Group Public Relations is the seventh-largest public relations firm in Colorado, and the company retains sister offices in New York and New Jersey, with affiliates in Atlanta and Tel Aviv.

The firm's focus is broad, covering everything from political strategy and governmental relations to product publicity and international media relations. The company has particular skills in the areas of real estate and information technology, as well as product publicity.

Freeman Group Public Relation's executive team includes (from left) Sharon Freeman, president; James Wall, executive vice president and partner; and Gerald Freeman, board chairman.

A Wealth of Talent

Each of the principal members of Freeman Group Public Relations brings distinct skills to the table. After 45 years in the field, Gerald Freeman's general business savvy is a highly valuable resource, and his vast experience in the public relations and marketing field means his contacts in local and national media are unmatched.

Sharon Freeman has been in public relations for more than 20 years in New York, New Jersey, and Colorado. In the Rocky Mountain region, she's known for her work with government and quasigovernmental bodies, political campaigns, and community relations.

Before joining the firm, Wall was a practicing attorney in downtown Denver, specializing in corporate transactions and complex offshore risk planning. Now a seasoned publicist and public relations strategist, he specializes in international public relations, focusing on companies in Colorado that are doing business in Europe.

"We characterize ourselves as a New York-style agency in the middle of Denver," says Gerald Freeman. "Our approach with the media is one of courteous aggression—we're creative, persistent, and results oriented. The bottom line is positive press, TV, and radio coverage for our clients."

"We're also very flexible—the media demands it," adds Wall. "By that, we mean that a well-thought-out strategy is quickly discarded if it isn't working. It's no use banging heads against a brick wall. Changing course midstream is a refined skill for the public relations professional, and it requires inventiveness and media savvy."

Wall's presence adds to the firm's flexibility. As a young, Eton-educated, British transplant, he brings a cross-cultural and cross-generational perspective that nicely balances Gerald Freeman's veteran New York approach. And Sharon Freeman's deft and highly effective political and community relations skills give the firm a unique depth of approach.

A Long List of Prestigious Clients

The firm's client list reflects the principals' mix of styles. Through the years, the Freemans have served some of the country's leading financial, insurance, and real estate companies, including Chubb Corporation; Lehman Brothers; Prudential Insurance Company; the Lefrak Organization, the nation's largest builder of multifamily housing; R.H. Macy-Shopping Center Division; Tishman Management Co., one of the country's major office building owners; and many more. Benjamin Moore Paint Company, Levelor Blinds, and Tyco Toy Corporation, the world's third-largest toy company (now a division of Mattel), have all been clients of Freeman Group Public Relations, and many remain

Freeman Group Public Relations opened its Denver office in 1992.

clients of the firm's sibling organization in New Jersey.

Recent and/or continuing Rocky Mountain region clients include such varied names as Asphalt Paving, Inc., a regional aggregate mining and road-building company; Bazar.net, a leading Russian Internet portal with corporate headquarters in Denver; BJ Adams & Company, a real estate brokerage leading the way in Aspen, Snowmass, and the Roaring Fork Valley; BrandMatrix, Inc., an Internet software company that solves the problems of brand control and retail channel conflict on the Web; and CT Power & Iceberg Enterprises, Inc., a provider of mobile rental refrigeration.

The firm's list of prestigious clients also includes Colorado Association of Commerce and Industry, Colorado's largest multi-industry association and a principal lobbying instrument for business; Denver West Realty, Inc., a major real estate owner and developer; the Gallin Company, the principal land and commercial developer in the Crested Butte area of Colorado; Jefferson Economic Council, a private/public partnership that promotes the economic development of Jefferson County, Colorado; Prostate Cancer Information Council, a national awareness organization for information surrounding prostate cancer; and Turner Construction Company-Denver Division, builders of the new Denver Broncos NFL Stadium, the State Correctional Facility in Sterling, Colorado, and the new atrium at Columbine High School.

Claudia Maniatis serves as account services director at the Freeman Group.

In his downtown office overlooking the majestic Colorado Rockies, Melvin E. Bush operates Insurance Design & Placement, Inc., a commercial insurance company he founded in 1993. The breathtaking view of the Front Range from his 24th-floor office is exactly what prompted Bush to move to Denver from St. Louis in 1983, when, during a visit, the mountains beckoned him to stay. ● In his early days in Denver, Bush worked as a security guard at night and on his insurance business by day, strategically launching another phase of the insurance career he has come to know and enjoy since 1973. Today, Insurance

Design & Placement—whose mission is to establish and maintain long-term relationships with its customers—has grown to become the largest minority-owned commercial-lines agency west of the Mississippi.

"It's been a very, very long road since when I started working in insurance independently in St. Louis in 1973," says Bush, company president. "But it's been very rewarding. My philosophy has always been if you stop getting better, you stop being good."

Melvin E. Bush serves as president of Insurance Design & Placement, Inc.

Success through Excellent Service

Since 1993, Insurance Design & Placement has seen revenues grow 32 percent annually, while in 1999 revenues soared a phenomenal 65 percent. The company specializes in the hospitality industry, providing all lines of commercial insurance coverage to a select market nationally and internationally—including restaurants, food distributors, and food manufacturers.

Bush's company is the exclusive agent for employment practice liability programs sold nationally to fast-food franchisees. "We now are ready to market the program nationally to all McDonald's and Burger King franchisees," says Bush, noting that Insurance Design & Placement has streamlined the application process to make it as efficient as possible. "We are licensed to write business insur-

Insurance Design & Placement is the exclusive agent for employment practice liability programs sold nationally to fast-food franchisees.

ance from New York to California to Texas."

While the hospitality industry is its niche, Insurance Design & Placement doesn't limit its commercial ventures. The company recently won the Super Bowl of insurance contracts locally—a bid to provide claims management and loss-control services for the Denver Broncos' new, $325 million stadium under construction near Mile High Stadium. The much-sought-after contract covers all workers' compensation claims and risk management services during the stadium's construction phase, when up to 1,500 workers descend

on the stadium as construction peaks toward an August 2001 opening.

Insurance Design & Placement also was named exclusive agent for the Hartford's Internet provider program, offering complete coverage for Internet service providers. The company was even prepared to handle any claims stemming from the highly publicized Y2K bug scheduled to hit at the turn of the century.

"The way we manage claims sets us apart from other companies," says Bush. "Our method of operation is to be proactive. We keep our clients informed along the way of

how a claim is progressing. And we follow up to make sure our clients' employees are satisfied. We don't wait for a complaint to come up; we get to them first."

Going that extra mile to keep communication lines open is key to Insurance Design & Placement's success. The company boasts a 96 percent customer retention rate. "Our clients tell us that our agency's service is what sets us apart and is what truly makes the difference to their bottom line," says Bush. Statistics show that clients who have been with Insurance Design & Placement for at least five years have had a reduction in their losses averaging 20 percent.

Another plus that keeps clients happy is Insurance Design & Placement's excellent rapport with insurance carriers, including such A-rated carriers as Safeco Insurance Co., Travelers Property Casualty, the Hartford,

Reliance National, AIG, Berkshire, and Seneca.

In an effort to bring clients the latest in technological advancement, Insurance Design & Placement reinvested profits into computer software and hardware for the agency. "We are confident our current setup is ready to handle our growth," says Bush.

International Growth, Local Commitment

Insurance Design & Placement's success in the hospitality industry prompted Bush to expand his business, forming two wholly owned subsidiaries, Global Transportation Insurance Services Inc. and Desirable Outcome Claims Services Inc. Global operates internationally, including Argentina, Brazil, Mexico, South Africa, and Nigeria, providing services to companies transporting products—covering everything from their

vehicles and cargo to the individual workers who perform the work.

Desirable Outcome Claims Services operates on a fee-for-services basis, providing claims management and loss-control services. "Our services are used by partially and fully self-insured risk management programs," says Bush.

Bush is not all business, however; he believes that, as a successful businessman in Denver, he should give back to the community. Bush is president of the Lower Downtown Rotary Club, and sits on the boards of directors of the Ronald McDonald House, Colorado Action for Healthy People, and Women's Bean Project. He also tutors students at the YMCA and provides career coaching at Manual High School. "I feel blessed to be able to give back to the community that has been so good to me," says Bush.

Insurance Design & Placement recently won the Super Bowl of insurance contracts locally—a bid to provide claims management and loss-control services for the Denver Broncos' new, $325 million stadium under construction near Mile High Stadium (top and bottom).

KeyBank/McDonald Investments Inc.

Cleveland, Ohio-based banking giant KeyCorp moved onto the Colorado landscape in 1993, lured by Colorado's strong economy and healthy banking industry. ● Key's first venture in the state was its acquisition of Home Federal Savings Bank in Fort Collins in June 1993. Other acquisitions followed, including Commercial Bancorporation of Colorado in March 1994 and Omnibancorp in September 1994. ● Today, Key is one of Colorado's largest and most rapidly growing financial institutions, and is an increasingly important market for its parent, KeyCorp, which is the 11th-largest bank-based financial services company in the United States, with assets of approximately $85 billion.

Key's roots date back to 1849, when Society for Savings of Cleveland, Ohio, was incorporated, and to 1825, when Commercial Bank of Albany, New York, was founded. In 1994, these banking pioneers merged to form KeyCorp, which today ranks 238th in the Fortune 500, based on total revenues. The company also ranks 93rd in the Forbes Super 100, based on composite rankings of sales, profits, assets, and market value. Of these values, Key placed 35th in assets and 88th in net profits.

Key companies provide investment management, retail and commercial banking, consumer finance, and investment banking products and services to individuals and companies throughout the United States. Key businesses deliver their products and services through facilities—including a network of about 2,500 ATMs—in 46 states. Colorado is among 13 states where Key offers retail banking services. Key employs more than 23,000 people, and maintains more than 3.8 million household and commercial clients.

Small-Business Innovations

Colorado, renowned for its entrepreneurial spirit and abundance of small businesses, is a healthy setting for Key's Small Business Services division. Small Business Services offers everything from business checking and lending programs to KeyPay Business, which allows small businesses to make payments easily and conveniently from any Touch-Tone phone—24 hours a day, seven days a week.

"Small business is our business, and we will continue our efforts toward understanding and meeting the needs and concerns of our customers," says Mike Butler, vice chairman of Small Business Services.

Among its small-business innovations, Key introduced the Key Solution Center, designed to provide small-business owners with instant access to a variety of tools and services through Key's Web site, www.key.com. "This is a one-stop solution center for small-business owners looking for help with accounting, sales, marketing, E-commerce, or human resources," says Butler. "They'll find it all on key.com."

Increasing Convenience through Technology

Key's technology has long been at the forefront of financial services. The company holds the distinction of being the first nationwide bank to link KeyCenter (branch), ATM, telephone, and PC/Internet transactions for instantaneous account information.

"This technology is changing the way people and business conduct commerce," says Robert W. Gillespie, Key chairman and chief executive. "It has great potential, but also great risks for those who are unable to keep up with it. I am proud of our Internet team for keeping Key more competitive—with far less budget to work with—than many other organizations."

Personalized Services

On the banking front, Key's Commercial Bank provides financial expertise, counsel, and customized solutions to help business clients reach their goals. Financing solutions are delivered to clients in such diverse industries as manufacturing, agriculture, construction, and international trade. The Commercial Bank's target market is composed of businesses reporting total annual sales

Key's headquarters is located in downtown Denver in the World Trade Center.

Key has locations throughout Colorado, including many in area grocery stores (left).

Greg Boushelle, small business relationship manager, visits a construction site (right).

Key employees are active in many community service activities, including Neighbors Make the Difference day each September (left and top right).

Key is the exclusive banking sponsor of the Colorado Avalanche (bottom right).

between $5 million and $250 million.

At Key PrivateBank, a team of experts identifies the long-term financial goals of its private banking and investing clients, and then makes recommendations about individualized plans for those businesses. For consumers, Key offers an assortment of products and services to meet changing needs, whether a customer is simply looking for an account to hold some extra cash or needs a long-term investment solution. Key also offers a range of on-line banking services.

Committed to Local Communities

Since 1996, Key has increased the number of its branches in the Colorado market from 27 to more than 40, and the number continues to grow. The expansion has included a number of bank locations inside King Soopers grocery store, offering customers even more convenience. A significant increase in Key's ATM network, including machines in 75 Total Petroleum locations, further increases customer access. Recently,

Key capped its Colorado expansion by establishing a headquarters in downtown Denver.

A Community Contributor

But all is not business at Key where, virtually every day, associates are volunteering in the community—tutoring children at a local school, serving meals to the hungry and homeless, or serving on nonprofit association boards of directors.

Every year, Key hosts Neighbors Make the Difference day, when thousands of Key employees spend much of the day making their communities better places. Among the numerous worthwhile organizations Key supports, the company has significant relationships with United Way and Habitat for Humanity International.

In 1999, Key, the Key Foundation, and Key employees gave nearly $5 million—40 percent of which was the Key employees' share—to United Way campaigns across the country. That same year, Key donated 14 homes in 11 major U.S. cities to Habitat for

Humanity International. The homes, valued at a total of $550,000, were the first step in Key's five-year program to contribute $2.5 million in properties to local Habitat organizations for rehabilitation.

Key's local presence in Colorado is further strengthened by its support for numerous area nonprofit and community groups. For example, Key makes significant contributions to the Denver Housing Redevelopment Project, a group that works with developers to make affordable housing a reality. Key also sponsors a new chapter of the Christmas in April program, providing both monetary and volunteer support for this upstart organization. And through its efforts with the Denver Metropolitan Homeless Initiative, Key has enabled the provision of numerous services to Denver's homeless population.

In every community it serves, Key looks to connect with organizations, events, and activities that are unique to that community. In Colorado, this initiative has led the company to establish partnerships with organizations

David McGrath

Len Williams is president of Key's Colorado district.

such as Colorado Ski Country USA, Denver Nuggets, Colorado Avalanche, Colorado's Ocean Journey aquarium, and Denver Art Museum.

McDonald Investments Inc.

McDonald Investments Inc., Key's investment banking and brokerage arm, ventured into Denver in 1999, setting up shop with two investment bankers. McDonald Investments quickly expanded with the acquisition of the Wallach Company to establish the largest investment banking operation in the area.

At corporate headquarters in Cleveland, Key executives took notice of the Denver success story, designating Denver the hub of the company's corporate finance activities west of Cleveland.

Key acquired McDonald Investments in late 1998 for $580 million in stock and cash. Since then, the investment banking unit has expanded from a large regional company to a national entity. In 1999, McDonald Investments assisted in 63 transactions—with a total value of $4.3 billion—in 30 states.

In Denver, McDonald Investments' transactions have included securing $210 million in financing for a privately held food retailer. McDonald Investments advised Lucent Technologies Inc. on a $105 million lease on its Highlands Ranch facility, and sole managed a $20 million follow-on public equity offering for Mallon Resources.

McDonald Investments' bankers provide financial advice and assist companies with stock offerings, mergers and acquisitions, debt

offerings, project financing, and private equity placements. The company has put together deals in such diverse sectors as industrial, real estate, consumer/retail, financial services, media/telecommunications, health care, and technology.

Impressive Rankings

McDonald Investments has been ranked by fund managers as one of America's best providers of investment research and analysis on U.S. midsize and small companies. In the *2000 Reuters Survey of U.S. Mid to Smaller Companies*, McDonald Investments was ranked 19th in the top 20 by representatives of the 200 largest institutional managers of active U.S. equity funds.

"We are very proud to be recognized by fund managers for our investment research," says Douglas Preiser, managing director. "This validates both our analysts' deep knowledge

of their target industries, and McDonald's traditional strength in small-cap and mid-cap companies."

The *Wall Street Journal* has also recognized McDonald Investments' research and analysis, ranking the company 16th of 220 firms, based on the number of Best on the Street Analyst awards earned by analysts.

"It's particularly meaningful to receive such a distinction from fund managers, an important client group for McDonald Investments," says Michael Hobbs, senior vice president. "It says that as investment professionals themselves, they respect and appreciate our ability to apply a critical eye to the companies and industries we cover."

"Key is committed to Colorado," says Len Williams, Colorado district president. "We are excited about the opportunity for growth here and our ability to give Colorado residents world-class financial services from local professionals."

David McGrath

Michael Hobbs serves as senior vice president of McDonald Investments.

1995-2001

1995	Xilinx Colorado
1996	Kimsey Electrical Contracting
1996	Lucent Technologies NetworkCare Knowledge Center
1996	SUPERVALU Inc.
1997	Aspen Petroleum Products
1997	Colorado Heart Imaging
1999	Clear Channel Colorado
1999	Level 3 Communications, Inc.

The unique corporate culture of Xilinx Colorado is evident the moment visitors walk through the doors: Indoor bike racks show that, for the outdoors-minded employees who ride their bicycles to work, management has provided a safe place to stow them. ● "We have a casual work environment here," says Kenn Perry, managing director. "We recruit top people in the high-tech industry to this area, and then keep them happy with a very competitive salary, a stock purchase program, and equity ownership in the company. Once somebody comes here to work, they usually don't leave."

Under a casual dress code, employees may wear shorts or jeans. They have complete flextime in which to do their jobs—any time, any day, just as long as the work gets done. Tuition is reimbursed 100 percent, and the company maintains an open-door policy all the way to the top levels of management. Xilinx also encourages balance between work life and home life.

Xilinx Colorado represents another in a series of innovations for the San Jose-based Xilinx, a leading innovator of complete programmable logic solutions. Xilinx revolutionized the industry in 1984 when it introduced the field programmable gate array (FPGA), and the company now commands more than half of the world market for devices that allow customers to reduce the time required to develop products for various industry segments, including computer, telecommunications, peripheral, networking, industrial control, instrumentation, high-reliability/military, and consumer markets.

Future of Growth

Xilinx Colorado has experienced tremendous growth since its opening in 1995. Having quickly outgrown its original Boulder plant, the company in 1999 broke ground on a 130,000-square-foot facility on a 60-acre campus in Longmont. The new building will be more than double the size of the Boulder facility, and will have room for some 400 employees, more than double the current staff of some 180.

"It will have a flagstone walking mall, a whole series of little ponds and rivers, a barbecue and camping area, a fishing pond for employees' children, and modem hook-ups outside so employees can use their laptops in a grove of aspens," says Perry. "We want this plant to capture the culture of Colorado and be a place that people will visit with their families on weekends."

An employee committee helped decide what to include in the new facilities, such as indoor recreational rooms, as well as bus service and bike paths that will offer alternative transportation.

An Industry Leader

But Xilinx is more than just a great place to work. The company's release of an unprecedented number of new products in 1999 not only positioned the firm as an industry leader, but boosted its bottom line to record revenues of $662 million, outpacing the industry growth rate. The publicly traded company employs about 1,600 people worldwide, and has manufacturing operations in San Jose and near Dublin, Ireland. A facility in Albuquerque develops CoolRunner complex programmable logic devices (CPLD).

Xilinx Colorado in 1999 introduced Internet reconfigurable logic (IRL) technology to its offerings, enabling customers to remotely reconfigure Xilinx's million-gat Virtex chips. The telecommunications and networking industries, in particular, welcomed the

Having quickly outgrown its original Boulder plant, Xilinx Colorado in 1999 broke ground on a 130,000-square-foot facility on a 60-acre campus in Longmont. The new building will be more than double the size of the Boulder facility.

Xilinx's new facility will replicate Colorado's culture.

innovation. About 65 percent of Xilinx's revenue comes from these rapidly changing markets.

The company's aggressive research and development strategy has established Xilinx as the leading innovator in programmable logic devices, or PLD technology, for consistently being first to market with new innovations. Xilinx exited 1999 with a 30 percent share of the PLD market.

Boulder is the hub of Xilinx's software development and Internet product offerings, but the company is expanding into new frontiers, says Perry, pointing to E-commerce as one of the latest areas of concentration. A core group of employees has been assigned to develop strategies and standards for Xilinx's E-commerce activities and the sale of Xilinx products over the Internet. On the information technologies front, Perry says Xilinx Colorado

will become the focus and delivery point for technical, architectural, and system excellence in the areas of E-commerce, LAN, WAN, telecommunications, core services, and S/W manufacturing and distribution.

"We also are establishing a long-term, balanced presence of customer services and support functions across the Silicon Valley and into the Boulder Valley," says Perry, explaining that the company offers a complete array of services, training, and support. Besides a frontline team, customers have access to customer support information systems.

Solutions for the Community

Xilinx's reputation as a solutions company goes beyond technology and extends into the Boulder Valley community, where the company and its

employees support dozens of local charities and civic activities. Xilinx provided computers to underprivileged children in Lafayette and to a hearing-impaired youngster. The company matches employee gifts to Toys for Tots, partners with the YMCA on a youth camping program, and supports Boulder Community Food Share.

Located along a Boulder bike path, Xilinx participates widely in Bike & Walk to Work Day activities, and adopted a stream along the bike path that employees keep clear of trash.

All that Xilinx does adds up to a corporate culture that goes beyond the workstation, and includes a manifest of virtues employees are expected to abide by, including customer service, respect, accountability, teamwork, integrity, and open communication. Concludes Perry, "At Xilinx, people enjoy their work."

Kimsey Electrical Contracting

Having worked on such marquee projects as the lighting of the Eisenhower Tunnel, the new Broncos Stadium, and an Intel fabrication plant, Denver's Kimsey Electrical Contracting's reputation is spreading as steadily as its body of work. From revenues of $4 million in 1996 to $14 million in 1999, with 2000 projections at approximately $47 million, Kimsey has grown rapidly. ● Vice President Stephen M. Kimsey leads the company with more than 25 years of electrical contracting experience to his credit. Kimsey Electrical's portfolio of projects includes everything from electrical work on the Southwest Corridor extension

of the Regional Transportation District's (RTD) light-rail system to the United Airlines Flight Training Center, Lockheed-Martin's fire alarm system, Cafe Odyssey, and the Nextel facility in Lonetree, Colorado. The company has also worked on projects ranging from downtown lofts and residential subdivisions to assisted living facilities for seniors. Kimsey Electrical helps move traffic by working on bustling highways such as the Boulder Turnpike and Interstates 25 and 70, where it has installed weather stations, light sensors, fiber-optic signage, and other technologies, laying a foundation for Colorado's highway system of the future.

A Strong Start

Kimsey Electrical, a division of Fischbach & Moore Electric Inc., has deep roots in the modernization of the American landscape. Fischbach & Moore, founded in New Jersey in 1918, was the creation of Rumanian immigrant Henry F.

Fischbach. In its early years, the growing entity was a key player in such historic projects as the lighting of the Holland Tunnel in New York in 1927 and the provision of electrical services to the United Nations Building in 1952. Shortly after that, the company worked on major projects at Los Angeles International Airport, the George Washington Bridge in New York, and the CBS Building in New York.

Among the other notable electrical projects in the company's historic portfolio are launch towers for NASA's *Saturn V* rocket at Cape Kennedy; World Trade Center; Chase Manhattan Bank; Chicago's Prudential Building; Lincoln Center in New York; Kennedy Center and Union Station in Washington, D.C.; and major sports complexes in Ohio and Missouri.

Through the decades, Fischbach & Moore grew into such a success story that corporate raiders took notice and acquired the company in 1990. In 1998, the company

returned to private hands after a team of executives led by then President and CEO James F. Kimsey took over the firm. In June 1998, Fischbach & Moore acquired Kimsey Electrical to manage its western operation.

Partnership in Action

In 1999, Fischbach & Moore joined forces with Philadelphia-based Exelon Infrastructure Services Inc. (EIS), a national infrastructure service provider. "This is a whole new way of looking at contracting service," says Kimsey. "Joining forces with EIS allows us to offer customers a new approach to contracting. With one phone call, they can get all their infrastructure needs—gas, electrical, telecommunications—a complete infrastructure designed specifically to meet their needs. This is our vision of the future—to do it all as a turnkey operation."

The partnership with EIS, an unregulated subsidiary of PECO Energy Company, makes Kimsey Electrical's 335-plus employee operation part of a team that includes a national workforce of some 5,000 people. EIS does business in 36 states and has revenues of approximately $500 million. Revenues are projected to grow to as high as $2 billion by the end of 2000.

EIS envisions being the nation's preferred provider of management, construction, operation, and maintenance services in the electric, gas, communication, commercial, and industrial markets. EIS only invites the best to join its network of infrastructure providers, tapping Fischbach & Moore because of its history of proven success and growth potential.

"We are now part of a team that is rebuilding the infrastructure in this country that was built in the 1940s," says Kimsey. "This expands our range of services to include not only electrical, but also gas, telecommunications, cable, and water utilities. It puts us at the forefront of providing the services that are expected to be totally deregulated in the next 10 years. We want to be the leader in this new approach to contracting."

Traditionally, large utilities have used internal resources or multiple contractors for projects, but the EIS partnership creates greater growth opportunities for Kimsey Electrical, which generally operates within a 250-mile radius of Denver, and has done projects in Texas and Wyoming.

The Light the House project, erected each year by Kimsey Electrical Contracting, has generated more than $2 million for the Ronald McDonald House.

Supporting Community Efforts

While being part of a national infrastructure revolution, Kimsey Electrical remains focused on its local roots and its commitment to the community. Each Christmas, Kimsey Electrical lights the Ronald McDonald House, where parents of children in nearby hospitals can stay for free, and sponsors the Light the House fund-raising campaign. For Light the House, Kimsey Electrical erects a strikingly lit outline of a house on the side of Mile High Stadium; donors are then encouraged to buy one of the 25,000 bulbs that light a red heart inside the house.

"The Light the House campaign has raised more than $2 million for the Ronald McDonald House," says Kimsey. "This is a campaign that is very close to our hearts and we will continue to support it for years to come."

Poised for the utility industry's coming changes and committed to professional excellence and community involvement, Kimsey Electrical Contracting has become a force in the Denver area and beyond.

Kimsey has worked on a variety of projects in the Denver area, including Safeway's dairy manufacturing facility (top left), the Nextel facility (top right), and the Regional Transportation District's Southwest Corridor Light Rail Line (middle and bottom).

Lucent Technologies NetworkCare Knowledge Center

At Lucent Technologies NetworkCare Knowledge Center, technicians with specialized skills in network operations keep their eyes on business operations around the world from a huge room they call the bunker. The center has been housed in a nondescript office building in Aurora, Colorado, since its founding in 1996; its bunker room is a tranquil space—lit by dozens of computer screens and desk lamps—featuring floor-to-ceiling maps, globes, and screens of data. From this room, dozens of highly trained technicians keep the networks of more than 70 major corporations operating 24 hours a day, seven days a week.

"We get about 12,000 alarms a day," says Hank Fore, vice president of Lucent's NetworkCare center. "The Internet is always on, and so is the center, 365 days a year."

The NetworkCare center opened in 1996 as part of Bell Labs, an offshoot of AT&T, to provide remote management and around-the-clock support for corporate networks. Companies range from start-ups to the well established. Emerging local exchange carriers have been a boon to the company, Fore says.

Meeting Technological Challenges

Today, the center serves some 70 companies, including such giants as Qwest Communications, that control a combined 20 percent of the wireless network market. Fore expects Lucent NetworkCare to double those numbers next year, as more start-up companies fuel demand among newly established carriers. Lucent NetworkCare is poised to meet all of these carriers' network needs with everything from network planning and integrating new technology to keeping a network operating at its full potential.

Lucent NetworkCare is also prepared to meet this challenge by offering everything from network administration, troubleshooting, and backup to network alarm management, problem diagnosis, and disaster recovery procedures, along with routine network moves, additions, and changes.

"Keeping a network operating at its full potential can sometimes overwhelm an in-house staff at a company," says Fore. "But we can provide the supplemental staffing and skills that a company needs."

A Dedicated Staff

Lucent NetworkCare in Aurora employs nearly 350 people, including a team affectionately known as the Jedi Warriors. Within the NetworkCare center, tier I technicians keep their eyes on the various network operations of the corporations they serve. This group receives the initial alarms and tries some basic solutions. If necessary, this group passes the issues along to a tier II group, which then goes to work to find solutions.

"If they're unable to fix it, that's when we bring in the Jedi Warriors," says Fore. "We keep 98 percent of the work right here, rather than handing it off elsewhere."

The center is part of a network of worldwide Lucent offices staffed by more than 600 technicians who coordinate virtually every network technology for companies around the globe. The Aurora location was home to the Y2K emergency center for the entire Lucent network on New Year's Eve 1999, although no problems emerged.

Lucent NetworkCare is the largest independent network-services provider in the world, with engineers and consultants stationed around the globe. Many of the world's largest companies, including more than 110 U.S.-based Fortune 500 companies, rely on Lucent NetworkCare to manage their complex networks. Major markets for Lucent's NetworkCare services and software solutions include financial services, health care, higher education, manufacturing, media, government, and service providers.

At Lucent Technologies NetworkCare Knowledge Center in Aurora, Colorado, technicians with specialized skills monitor customer networks around the world (this page and opposite).

performance of today's complex networks." In addition to monitoring, Lucent NetworkCare analyzes and performs diagnostics of network performance to identify areas where service can be improved.

"We fully understand multivendor networking, and, while our competitors rely on other companies to provide this function, we have a direct services approach that provides the customer a single point of contact from stronger operations control and customer satisfaction," says Akers, explaining that a maintenance and management service manager is assigned to handle all of a company's service issues. "This is especially critical as customers expand into several different regions at one time."

Giving Back to the Community

Wanting to be a part of the community where it is located, the NetworkCare center's sleek interior design is open to the public, and annually attracts some 300 visitors who are awed by the artwork that changes colors, as well as other high-tech features. "We look high-tech because we are high-tech—even down to our artwork, which is by Colorado artists," says Fore.

But welcoming the community into the facility is only part of what the center gives back to the community. "We're a high-tech company with heart," says Fore. "We support many local charities and organizations. Our employees have even taken days off to help build homes as part of Habitat for Humanity. We definitely get out of this bunker and into the community with our work."

Ensuring Customer Satisfaction

In today's economy, nobody has the time or the resources to create and maintain a staff that will oversee their entire network," says Jeff Akers, president of technical support services. "So it makes sense for companies to outsource that part of their business and let us do it for them. We have the people, the processes, and the tools that companies need to maximize the

As the world's leading wholesale food distribution company and the nation's 10th-largest food retailer, SUPERVALU Inc. strives to be America's shopping cart. The more than $20 billion company, based in Minneapolis, accounts for more than 15 percent of the nation's food distribution business, supplies some 3,500 supermarkets, and is a partial supplier to some 2,600 stores in 48 states. SUPERVALU has approximately 85,000 employees, and operates a distribution system comprised of 36 regional distribution centers across the nation, including one in the Denver suburb of Aurora.

In addition, SUPERVALU operates some 1,100 corporate-owned stores with such banner names as Shoppers Food Warehouse, Shop 'n' Save, Save-a-Lot, Metro, Scott's Foods, Laneco, Farm Fresh, and Hornbacher's. Representing the company in the Denver area are Cub Foods and Bigg's.

A Rich History

The SUPERVALU of today is a far cry from its original store. The company was founded in Minneapolis as B.S. Bull, Newell & Harrison Co. The SUPERVALU name itself came onto the grocery landscape in 1942, when the company dissolved its franchise with the Independent Grocery Association and formed a group of stores with an extensive program of services to retailers, as well as an emphasis on nationally advertised brand names.

Centralizing Customer Service

Customer service has always been crucial to SUPERVALU's success. The company's food distribution follows a simple formula and offers three tiers of private-label choices. Through its Preferred Selections, the company offers top-notch, premium food and food-related products, and through such labels as Flavorite, HomeBest, and Richfood, it offers a broad spectrum of brand-name items. SUPERVALU makes high-quality, inexpensive products under such private labels as Bi-Rite and Shoppers Valu.

In 1996, Russell E. Schmuhl, director of customer service for SUPERVALU/Aurora, and a SUPERVALU team undertook the acclaimed Advantage project, an extensive study to create new, more efficient methods of distribution and customer service. Results of that project included a centralized nationwide system at the SUPERVALU Customer Service Center in Aurora. Early on, customers were a little reluctant to turn their needs over to a centralized location, but a market research study indicated the system was working well, giving SUPERVALU high marks for professionalism and thorough execution.

At the center, the company's some 185 highly skilled employees handle the nation's food transactions with courtesy. They handle calls from across the nation and have access to the company's mainframe to process financial transactions. In addition, they employ a high-tech call tracking and problem resolution system, and have internal technical support responsible for keeping the system humming.

"We're serious about the help part of our mission," Schmuhl says. "Anyone who calls in here is greeted by friendly, well-trained customer service professionals, and they can be sure that they have technology on their side to ensure their particular problems or orders are handled promptly and completely. We even have our own generator in case of power outages and a backup call center. We also direct inbound calls to a third-party partner facility in La Junta, Colorado. We truly are a professional problem-solving organization."

As a one-stop shopping distributor, SUPERVALU offers its grocery partners access to retail business consultants who assist with everything from payroll and advertising issues to bakery and deli or meat counter presentations. "We'll even plan their parking lot if that's what they need," says Schmuhl. "Our consulting depends on their needs. Our mission is to do what we can to help them to be more profitable."

Overall, the Advantage project has strengthened SUPERVALU's position as one of the nation's premier food distributors by creating a supply system that delivers goods at a lower cost to grocery clients and even to chain giants such as Kmart. Small to medium-sized grocers, who comprise the bulk of SUPERVALU's clients, have found

SUPERVALU Inc.'s Customer Service Center is located in the Denver suburb of Aurora.

the Advantage project especially helpful to their bottom lines, and are able to translate those savings into lower prices for their own customers.

"This project was advantageous to our independent niche and grocers in rural areas who were struggling," says Schmuhl. "We can even offer them further incentive through activity-based sell—ABS—which offers product promotion, streamlined delivery schedules, and product ordering."

At the SUPERVALU Customer Service Center in Aurora, the company's some 185 highly skilled employees handle the nation's food transactions with courtesy.

Growth and Giving

As the grocers' profits go, so goes SUPERVALU's growth. Since 1997, the company has grown into a $23 billion company, with sales growing at a rate of nearly 4 percent annually.

"Gains in sales and profits were due, in large part, to the success of our independent retailers, the most savvy food marketers in the nation," says Mike Wright, chairman, CEO, and president. "These world-class entrepreneurs continually fine-tune their operations, update their facilities, execute the latest in retail innovations, and satisfy their customers every day."

Just as store owners pass SUPERVALU's savings on to their own customers, the company is passing the benefits of its growth on to the community. At SUPERVALU's Aurora facility, for example, employees regularly volunteer to help local organizations, including assisting youth in Junior Achievement, making Christmas merrier for low-income children at the nearby Clyde Miller Elementary School, or building trails in Colorado's wilderness.

"We also work closely with Aurora Community College, which provides training for some of our workers and supplements our workforce," says Schmuhl. "Our people will always pull together where there's a need, whether it's for our customers or for our community."

Colorado Heart Imaging

Colorado Heart Imaging (CHI) serves thousands of people who exercise regularly, don't smoke, get annual checkups, and watch what they eat, yet are often among the millions of Americans who suffer from some form of cardiovascular disease— many of whom are unaware of their heart condition. Unfortunately for 150,000 Americans every year, a fatal heart attack is the first and only indication that a problem exists. CHI was founded in June 1997 to help reverse the trend in the Rocky Mountain region by screening patients to detect early heart disease. ● "We all have known apparently healthy people

develop an unexpected heart attack or stroke, often in their prime years," says Dr. James Ehrlich, medical director of CHI. "Risk factors cannot tell us who has early atherosclerosis, or plaque, the leading cause of death in America. Most of the previously healthy patients residing in coronary care units would have had an unremarkable cholesterol level and a normal treadmill test one month before their devastating coronary event," Ehrlich states. This is where advanced detection technology comes in—if detected early, coronary disease can be slowed, stopped, or even reversed by modern therapy, while admissions to coronary care can be avoided.

Electron Beam Tomography: A Breakthrough Medical Advance

Ehrlich and radiologist Dr. Robert Seigel opened CHI as the region's first center for the early, noninvasive detection of heart disease. CHI uses electron beam tomography (EBT), a state-of-the-art imaging technology, to detect coronary artery disease in its early stages, at a time when preventive strategies are the most successful.

EBT is an ultrafast CT scanner that is uniquely able to capture clear pictures of the moving heart. The entire procedure takes about 10 minutes, and is noninvasive (no needles or dyes) and safe. Patients simply take a couple of deep breaths while lying on a nonclaustrophobic table.

The resulting images reveal the presence and amount of calcium, a proven indicator of early coronary disease and the most powerful predictor of future heart attack episodes. Staff physicians interpret results, and appropriate treatment is recommended to patients and referring doctors. Minor amounts of plaque are often addressed by lifestyle modification, such as diet and exercise, or further attention to risk factors. More substantial calcium scores may require specific therapy, including plaque-stabilizing medications. With extensive disease, further testing by a cardiologist looking for hidden obstruction is recommended. Many patients, however, leave with the peace of mind that comes with discovering plaque-free arteries.

A heart scan is appropriate for middle-aged men and women as a screen for heart disease. Anyone with risk factors—such as high cholesterol, a family history of early

coronary disease, diabetes, hypertension, smoking history, sedentary lifestyle, or obesity—may also benefit from a heart scan. Many of the leading university-based preventive heart centers, including the Mayo Clinic, UCLA, Stanford, and Johns Hopkins, routinely use the ultrafast heart scan to diagnose the early stages of heart disease. EBT is FDA approved and was named by the American Heart Association as one of the top 10 advances in cardiology in 1999.

Ehrlich is the medical codirector for heart imaging centers in Washington, D.C., and Houston, and consults at other sites nationwide. More than 500 Colorado physicians have had their own hearts tested at CHI, and many have made major lifestyle changes or are taking specific medications to prevent their own first heart attack. "I can't imagine any other 10-minute test having such a dramatic impact on so many people," comments Ehrlich.

The procedure is particularly attractive to the intelligent, proactive, health-conscious citizen. Doctors, however, are usually reactive in nature—waiting for symptoms of heart disease before initiating treatment. This is

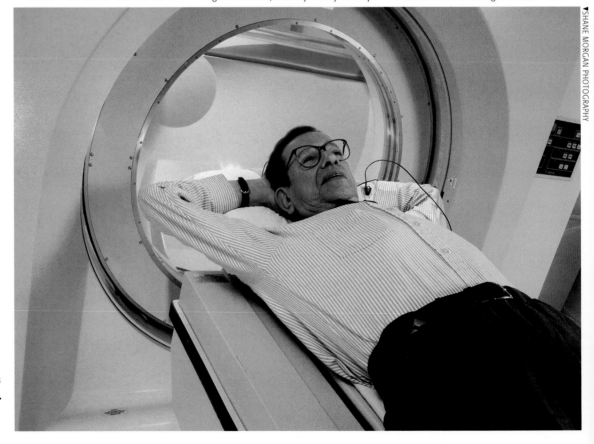

A heartscan at Colorado Heart Imaging has great impact upon thousands. Here Former Senator Paul Simon receives his first indication of severe heart disease. Simon underwent a multivessel bypass a few weeks later.

SEVERE CORONARY ARTERY CALCIFICATION

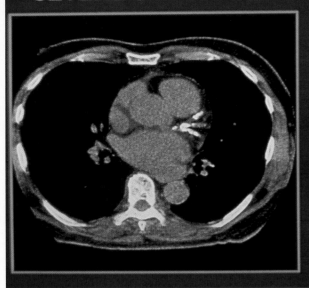

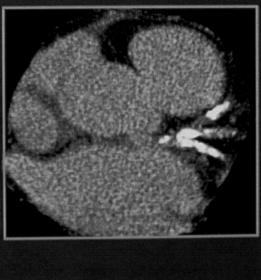

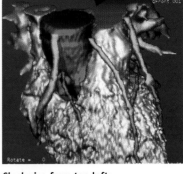

Clockwise from top left:
Viewing actual images of coronary arteries is possibly the best way to motivate positive lifestyle changes.

Colorado Heart Imaging performs noninvasive 3D coronary angiograms as a selective alternative to invasive cardiac catheterizations.

CHI uses electron beam tomography (EBT), a state-of-the-art imaging technology, to detect coronary artery disease in its early stages, at a time when preventive strategies are the most successful.

UltraFast CT is frequently the subject of national print and television coverage, including this article in a recent edition of *Newsweek.*

unfortunate because 30 percent of patients do not survive their first manifestation of the disease. "Unfortunately, doctors are not generally rewarded for prevention, and our managed care system is dramatically skewed toward intervention when symptoms are already present," asserts Ehrlich. "This tool [EBT] allows us to precisely identify the people who can most benefit from newer advances in preventive therapy."

Other Services at Colorado Heart Imaging

CHI also offers lung scans for the early detection of lung disease. Suitable for smokers—current and past—the procedure takes an extra two minutes and is often combined with a heart scan and pulmonary function testing. The EBT lung scan is capable of detecting a

tumor the size of a few grains of rice, at a time when cure rates are very high. "Lung cancer is the number one cancer killer," Ehrlich notes. "Unfortunately, the usual way people find out they have lung cancer is from a chest X-ray or by symptoms. The majority of individuals will not survive five years if the tumor is discovered that late." Other imaging services include total body scans, quantitative CT bone densitometry, and noninvasive coronary angiography, which can replace more invasive cardiac catheterization in suitable patients. Sometime in 2001, the center plans to offer virtual

colonoscopy, replacing uncomfortable scopes for many who simply need a screen for polyps and colon cancer.

CHI offers access to the best resources in prevention, an important service that includes consultation with leading experts in cardiology, pulmonary medicine, and cholesterol issues. In addition, arrangements have been made with companies offering sophisticated lipid testing, specialized antioxidants, and cholesterol-lowering medications and fibers. CHI's Web site, www.coloradoheart.com, is continually updated, alerting consumers to newer strategies in disease prevention.

Checking Your Vessels

Are you headed for a heart attack despite your low cholesterol? A $400 test makes it easier to find out.

APRIL 6, 1998 NEWSWEEK

By Geoffrey Cowley

WHEN YOUR CHOLESTEROL IS in the stratosphere and slicing bread makes your chest ache, you know you have a problem. Unfortunately, arterial disease doesn't always present such clear warnings. For some 150,000 Americans a year, the first and only sign of clogged arteries is a fatal heart attack. Are you headed for trouble despite your seeming good health? A new test— the Ultrafast CT scan—could make finding out a lot easier. The new scan can detect heart disease at its earliest and most treatable stages. And because the procedure is quick, cheap and noninvasive, it could become as common as mammography, and equally effective at saving lives.

The surest way to measure arterial blockage is through invasive procedures such as coronary angiography and intravascular ultrasound. But no one would suggest using those tests to screen healthy people. They cost $3,000 to $5,000 and involve threading a catheter from the groin up into the chest to examine the vessels that feed the heart. The new scanning procedure, developed by Imatron Inc. of South San Francisco, Calif., costs only $350 to $500 and is far less tricky. The patient simply lies on a table for five minutes with a doughnut-shaped scanner surrounding his chest. Like a conventional CT scan, the device uses beams of electrons to create interior images. But because it works at least seven times faster than a conventional CT scan, the pictures it generates aren't blurred by the motion of the heart and blood. By analyzing

images of the coronary arteries, a technician can determine how much calcium they contain—and that score provides a good indication of how badly they're clogged.

If the blockage looks severe, a cardiologist will perform the more invasive tests before prescribing angioplasty or bypass surgery. "To pinpoint a blockage, you still need an angiogram," says one specialist. But if the Ultrafast scan reveals, say, a 20 percent blockage in a seemingly healthy person, that person can attack the problem—with drugs or through diet and exercise—before it attacks his heart.

Only 40 U.S. clinics currently offer the Ultrafast CT scan, and because it's so new, few insurers cover the cost. But that's likely to change as researchers confirm its diagnostic power. In one ongoing study, doctors at New York's St. Francis Hospital have run the test on 1,172 symptom-free volunteers and followed them for periods of three to four years. The latest results, to be presented in Atlanta this week at a meeting of the American College of Cardiology, suggest that the Ultrafast CT scan gauges heart-attack risk 10 times more reliably than a cholesterol test. "The accuracy is unprecedented," says Dr. Alan Guerci, director of research at St. Francis. "Our findings suggest this could become the primary screening tool for coronary artery disease."

Mass screening of healthy adults would be a costly proposition, even at $400 a head. But if people acted on the results, the effort could be well worth the money. ■

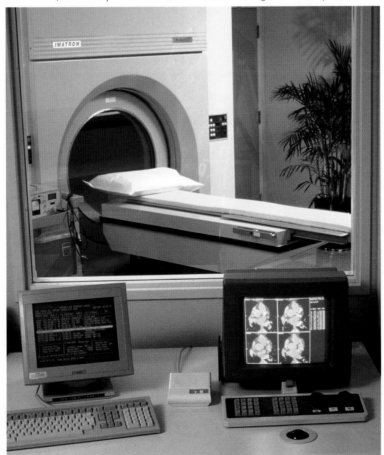

Aspen Petroleum Products has been supplying high-quality fuel additives to domestic and foreign markets since 1997. But the company's mission runs far deeper than manufacturing products that improve gasoline and diesel quality. In keeping with President Terrance Tschatschula's commitment to improving the quality of life for people around the world, the Denver company is applying environmental lessons learned in the United States to other countries worldwide. ● Among Aspen Petroleum's ambitious projects is the company's work with the government of Jalisco. This project focuses on reducing hydrocarbon and carbon monoxide emissions pouring from the cars in the crowded city of Guadalajara.

Better Health through Transfer of Technology

Tschatschula's history of working in developing nations dates back to 1993, when he served as technical adviser for the Ecuadoran government's campaign to supply unleaded gasoline in Quito, the country's capital. The government was gravely concerned about studies showing that airborne lead reduces the IQ of children and causes other health problems—a problem that was magnified by the rarefied air in the mountain city of Quito, 9,000 feet above sea level—and Aspen Petroleum was poised to find answers. "The transfer of technology is the first step in a developing country's march toward progress," says Tschatschula.

Solutions, however, are only worth pursuing if they can be carried out economically—and that is where the rest of Aspen Petroleum's mission comes into play. The company's philosophy is to balance the need for a safe and healthy environment with countries' social and economic development.

In Chile, for example, to the south of resort city La Serena, Aspen Petroleum is eliminating mercury-tainted material from precious metals mines. Chilean miners have used the silvery metal to extract gold from ore—an environmental danger, as the process left behind trace amounts of mercury. Aspen Petroleum intends to clean up the mining waste, remove the mercury, and return the property to its natural condition. At the same time, the project is economically viable, as Aspen Petroleum is also extracting precious metals that the miners' original mercury-based process left behind.

Fuel Additives for Added Safety

Aspen Petroleum is also taking its knowledge of fuel additives to eastern Europe. In an $8 million project, the company is dismantling and transporting a small oil refinery from the gulf coast of the United States to the Black Sea town of Varna. The operation will supply unleaded gasoline, fuel oil, diesel, asphalt, and liquefied petroleum gas from the processing of 25,000 barrels of crude oil per day. Aspen Petroleum will hold an equity interest in the refinery and will provide the fuel additives for the refinery products, which will be sold at Bulgaria's leading service stations.

Fuel additives are at the heart of Aspen Petroleum's business. The company currently manufactures 500,000 pounds of high-molecular-weight polyolefin detergents each year. The detergents are sold to aftermarket automotive suppliers—such as local auto parts stores—and to commercial fleet users.

And, while Aspen Petroleum's products may be found on the shelves of neighborhood auto parts stores, the Denver company is touching the world and expanding for the future with economically and environmentally viable projects.

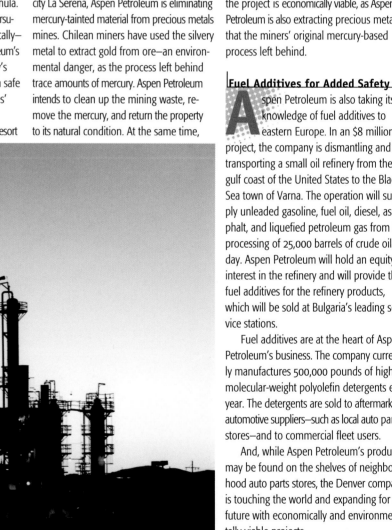

Terrance Tschatschula serves as president of Aspen Petroleum Products.

Aspen brings clean environmental projects to developing countries.

To take the pulse of a city, turn on the radio. In Denver, chances are one in three that you've tuned into a Clear Channel Colorado station—KBCO-FM, KBPI-FM, KHOW-AM, KOA-AM, KRFX-FM, KTCL-FM, KTLK-AM, or KISS-FM. From rock to talk to disc jockeys, Clear Channel Colorado has something for everybody. The company's eight radio stations have defined Denver's emotional moments, main events, and rites of passage for decades. ● Clear Channel Colorado is the Denver area's premier radio company, covering the spectrum of popular tastes in music, sports, and talk shows. Its parent

company—San Antonio-based Clear Channel Communications, Inc.—is a global leader in the out-of-home advertising industry, with radio and television stations and outdoor displays in some 40 countries.

Clear Channel Communications operates some 900 radio and 19 television stations in the United States, and has equity interests in more than 240 radio stations worldwide. Clear Channel also operates more than 700,000 outdoor advertising displays internationally, including billboards, street furniture, and transit panels.

Although a relative newcomer to the Denver market, Clear Channel Colorado has acquired eight long-standing radio stations whose sounds have been part of Denver's cultural landscape for some time. The company also owns signs at Denver International Airport and freestanding directory kiosks at shopping malls. With some 350 employees, Clear Channel's Denver office is the hub of a radio operation with spokes in Colorado Springs; Fort Collins, Wyoming; and the Dakotas.

Ratings Leader

Arbitron ratings—data compiled from the responses of people paid to listen to the radio and fill out diaries, jotting down every time they switch stations and how long they listen to each—indicate

Clear Channel Colorado radio station KOA-AM recently hosted a client party at Mile High Stadium.

that the eight Clear Channel stations garner more audience share than any other radio company in Denver. Clear Channel reaches ("reach" is the total number of people in the course of a week who listen for 15 minutes or more) more than half the Denver population during the course of a week. Clear Channel's usual share ("share" is how many people are listening at a given time) of listeners

is around 35 percent, far outpacing its nearest competitor, Jefferson Pilot.

Clear Channel came to Denver in May 1999 when it acquired eight Jacor radio stations. In August 2000, Clear Channel merged with radio giant AM FM, formerly known as Chancellor Broadcasting.

Despite ownership changes, the eight radio stations now in the Clear Channel family have remained relatively stable in terms of leadership, talent, formats, and ratings. The stations are run by two executives with long, successful radio careers in Denver, Lee Larsen and Don Howe, both of whom are vice presidents and general managers. Larsen and Howe divide the stations and territories, and have a philosophy of researching, responding, and sticking with what works.

"Listener loyalty is important to us, absolutely," says Larsen, a Denver radio executive since 1983. He manages Clear Channel's three Denver AM stations, as well as operations in other Colorado cities and Wyoming. "The stations that are successful stay in their formats. In any town, those are the stations you've heard of and are familiar with. For example, KBCO hasn't changed its rock music format in 20 years because it's been very successful."

Format changes happen infrequently—once every few years, and only if audience ratings slip. The last major format change at a Clear Channel station occurred in September

2000, when the company took jazz station KHIH off the air and moved it to streaming radio on the Internet. The old KHIH slot—95.7 FM—became a contemporary hits station with new call letters.

"We dropped the jazz format from KHIH because it was not garnering enough audience," Larsen says. "We thought, let's keep KHIH alive for those people who really like it. Let's experiment and put it on the Web so that some people can still follow it.

"Denver is a very sophisticated, extremely competitive radio market," Larsen adds. "Some of the best radio in the country is right here." He cites Boulder-based KBCO as a radio station that clicks with the Denver/Boulder

market, but would be hard to duplicate anywhere else.

"KBCO resonates with this city because of the high education level of the population here, and because of the lifestyle people have in Colorado—very outdoor oriented, active in both winter and summer," says Larsen. "KBCO understands the tastes of the population of this part of the country. You could pick up KBCO and put it in Cleveland, and I don't think it would work there. The other stations are all extremely good in their formats, whether it's talk or rock and roll. They are extremely well executed, and the level of talent at each of those stations is as good as you can find in the market. Listeners have many

Clear Channel radio stations share in the fun with their listeners.

other choices, which are also very good. So you have to remain very much on top of your game in this market, or listeners will go elsewhere."

Variety characterizes the eight Clear Channel stations. FM formats range from classic rock to adult-oriented alternative and rock. KBPI plays alternative music geared toward a younger male audience.

The three AM stations have their definite niches: KOA–"Colorado's most listened-to station"–broadcasts news and sports with talk thrown in. KOA's *Colorado's Morning News* focuses on in-depth coverage of hot news stories and topics, from forest fires near Boulder to Broncos, Rockies, and University of Colorado games. The afternoon lineup features Rush Limbaugh and *Sports Zoo.*

KHOW is Clear Channel's Denver talk station, featuring the topics of the day or week. KTLK covers business and sports, with *Business for Breakfast* offering information about the stock market, the top companies in Colorado and the country, the movers and shakers of the business world, and some sports.

Clear Channel owns the maximum number of radio stations allowed by law in the Denver market. Future expansion isn't a possibility unless the law changes. That means executives must strive to maintain top standing with the existing eight stations in their group.

"If we had more stations, we would look for more formats," Larsen says. "We don't have more stations, so we plan to hold steady with the current formats. But we don't know what the competition will do or how well a station might be doing a year from now. Music tastes change. As music changes, we might want to tweak our formats or change our radio stations.

One of the largest events in Colorado, KBCO's Kinetics starts with a parade (this page and opposite top).

This doesn't necessarily mean a wholesale format change, but we would modify our music to keep up with the tastes."

Larsen describes his business as "creating a partnership between listeners and advertisers." His job is to get as many people to listen as possible. "The measure is the audience: How big is the audience? What are the demographics of that audience?" adds

Larsen. "That's what you turn around and market to the advertisers."

"Advertisers are the ultimate payoff," says Larsen. "They don't want to pay us if we don't have enough listeners or the demographics they want. There are two things we do with audience and advertisers—we respond. If I tried to put a radio station on the air, say a talk station, that expressed my view of the world, that could be suicidal. You don't sit here and manipulate how things are going to go. What we do is respond to listeners and what they want, and we try to keep up with them. We try to stay as close as we can to them.

"If we're really stuck for an idea, we might try to get out in front of the audience. We'll say, 'Let's try this and see how they respond.' But for the most part, we do research all the time on what music is popular, what talk hosts are popular, what people want to hear on the radio, how much news do they want mixed with how much sports, how much weather, how much traffic. All we do is try to understand the audience and respond to them.

"As far as the advertisers are concerned, we try to make sure we know to whom they want to advertise. And if they have changed their target audience, we have to bear that in mind and say, 'Gee, that's who is going to pay the bills. What do they listen for?'

"If advertisers tend to move one way or another, we have to put that into our thinking. Basically, we try to respond and be there with the best that we have. If you ran a restaurant, you wouldn't put a menu together based

on your tastes, but on the tastes of your clientele. The ultimate test of how well a restaurant does is how many people come back and eat there. The ultimate test of a radio station is how many people come back and keep listening," Larsen says.

Technological Advances

Clear Channel keeps up with technology advances, putting all eight stations on streaming radio on the Internet. Matt Meehan, KOA promotions director, says Clear Channel uses the Internet as a marketing tool to help promote its stations and involve its advertisers.

Meehan feels certain that the Internet won't replace "real" radio, any more than CDs replaced radio or television replaced the film medium. "I switch back and forth between streaming radio and real radio," Meehan says. "A lot of office buildings downtown cannot pick up radio stations within their walls. There is a way to tell how many people are listening on streaming radio. We get huge numbers of downtown office listeners to streaming radio during games."

There will always be a place for radio, which will keep reinventing itself, just as it has with every technological advance, according to Larsen. "There is a proliferation of media, giving consumers more and more choices," Larsen says. "Radio has to keep up. That's where the level of professionalism must keep growing.

"We face constant evolution of communications technology. We always have to

respond to it. It's not how neat the device is, it's what comes out of the device that matters. We must constantly strive to have unique personalities, unique information, unique presentation.

"Anybody can play the same music we play. But how you package it together with who hosts it, what kind of fun you put in, is what matters. How you localize what you do,

how you make your station mean something to its community, how you involve your community in the news, traffic, weather, charitable causes, and recreational events—you need to be connected to your audience.

"That's why radio has survived over the years, despite television, audiotapes, and CDs," Larsen concludes. "It will continue to find ways to reinvent itself."

Some listeners will do anything to win a prize.

Level 3 Communications, Inc.

Level 3 Communications, Inc. is making history in the telecommunications industry by constructing the world's first upgradeable international communications network completely optimized for Internet Protocol (IP) technology. The company's fiber optic network is designed to be one of the world's most advanced communications platforms, and includes intercity networks and undersea cables connecting 77 cities in the United States, Europe, and Asia. In addition, Level 3 has built advanced technology gateways where communications-intensive customers physically locate and directly

connect their own servers and equipment to Level 3's advanced broadband network.

"Level 3's goal in life is not to be everything to everybody, but to succeed at what we do best—to allow our customers to communicate using bandwidth that leverages the advantages of ever improving technology," says James Crowe, CEO. "Ultimately, we will all see the benefits.

"The traditional phone networks built over the past century were designed as voice networks," Crowe continues. "And they extended the reach of our ears around the world. Now, we are entering a new era of visual communications—extending the reach of our eyes. The Internet is only the beginning."

Level 3 believes it will be able to continuously lower the cost of moving information by as much as 50 percent per year, bringing to the communications industry the kind of annual price-performance improvements previously seen in the computing industry.

A Quick Rise to Success

An engineer by training, Crowe held senior positions with Morrison Knudsen Corp. and Peter Kiewit Sons', Inc. before founding MFS Communications. In 1993, Crowe took MFS public. At the time of its $14.3 billion merger with WorldCom in 1996, MFS had become the largest competitive local carrier in the United

States and Europe. Following the merger, Crowe served as chairman of WorldCom. In 1997, he assumed the leadership of a diverse group of companies that would become Level 3. Crowe reshaped the group into a single company with a core focus on communications and information services.

Level 3 chose Colorado's Front Range as the location of its worldwide headquarters, constructing its campus complex in Broomfield's Interlocken Advanced Technology Park. The company opened its 42-acre corporate headquarters in November 1999, and became the third-largest corporation in Colorado in less than a year. Level 3 continues to be one of the region's fastest-growing employers, with approximately 2,500 of the company's 6,000 employees housed at the Broomfield campus.

Crowe says that Level 3 chose to locate in the Convergence Corridor because of Colorado's reputation as one of the fastest-growing, most important centers of technology and communications in the country. A company-sponsored study also revealed that the metro area had what the company needed: a skilled workforce, a quality lifestyle, an international airport, and community support and infrastructure.

"The results of the survey indicated that the Denver area not only ranked at or near the top with the kinds of employees Level 3 sought, but also had no negatives," says Crowe. "Clearly it was the right choice, as we have exceeded our recruiting goals in a very tight labor market."

At Level 3, employees are also owners and

Level 3 Communications, Inc. opened its 42-acre corporate headquarters in November 1999, and became the third-largest corporation in Colorado in less than a year.

are encouraged to think like owners willing to take balanced risks. Employees benefit from a unique stock option program in which options are worthless if Level 3 underperforms the market, as measured by the Standard & Poor's 500 Index, but are worth more than standard options if they outperform the market.

"Ownership is the foundation on which we build innovation, and it is the essence we live and breathe as we grow Level 3," says Crowe. "All employee-owners must share in our success. It is the caliber of our people—their entrepreneurial spirit and their drive—that will determine whether we are merely successful or whether we usher in a new era in communications."

Better Service at a Lower Cost

Today, Level 3 provides services for telecommunications and communications-intensive companies—those that operate a significant portion of their business over Web-based networks. These are companies with a high demand for moving vast amounts of information—capacity requirements that, on average, are doubling every four to six months. Level 3's advanced IP network, which is built to be continuously upgraded as technology evolves, enables business customers to benefit from the lower cost and service offerings made possible by IP technology.

Level 3 is not alone in touting its commitment to the telecommunications revolution, its mission, and its corporate strategy. As *USA Today* has stated, Level 3 is "a dream team with a dream network and a killer business plan."

On April 3, 2000, Level 3 was inducted into the permanent research collection of the Smithsonian Institution for its leadership in the information revolution and for its historic achievement of building "the world's first upgradeable international fiber optic network to be completely optimized for Internet Protocol technology, helping to stimulate the biggest change in communications technology in 100 years."

Level 3 Communications' business sense—in tandem with its technological innovations and implementations—provides the company's customers with the opportunity to reap the full benefits of innovations in communications technology.

Level 3's gateway technicians provide operational support.

The Executive Briefing Center gives visitors an opportunity to see how Level 3's operations are monitored in the Network Operations Center (NOC).

The NOC is the nerve center that monitors the company's entire fiber optic network in North America, Europe, and Asia.

Towery Publishing, Inc.

Beginning as a small publisher of local newspapers in the 1930s, Towery Publishing, Inc. today produces a wide range of community-oriented materials, including books (Urban Tapestry Series), business directories, magazines, and Internet publications. Building on its long heritage of excellence, the company has become global in scope, with cities from San Diego to Sydney represented by Towery products. In all its endeavors, this Memphis-based company strives to be synonymous with service, utility, and quality.

A Diversity of Community-Based Products

Over the years, Towery has become the largest producer of published materials for North American chambers of commerce. From membership directories that enhance business-to-business communication to visitor and relocation guides tailored to reflect the unique qualities of the communities they cover, the company's chamber-oriented materials offer comprehensive information on dozens of topics, including housing, education, leisure activities, health care, and local government.

In 1998, the company acquired Cincinnati-based Target Marketing, an established provider of detailed city street maps to more than 200 chambers of commerce throughout the United States and Canada. Now a division of Towery, Target offers full-color maps that include local landmarks and points of interest, such as recreational parks, shopping centers, golf courses, schools, industrial parks, city and county limits, subdivision names, public buildings, and even block numbers on most streets.

In 1990, Towery launched the Urban Tapestry Series, an award-winning collection of oversized, hardbound photojournals detailing the people, history, culture, environment, and commerce of various metropolitan areas. These coffee-table books highlight a community through three basic elements: an introductory essay by a noted local individual, an exquisite collection of four-color photographs, and profiles of the companies and organizations that animate the area's business life.

To date, nearly 90 Urban Tapestry Series editions have been published in cities around the world, from New York to Vancouver to Sydney. Authors of the books' introductory essays include two former U.S. presidents—Gerald Ford (Grand Rapids) and Jimmy Carter (Atlanta); boxing great Muhammad Ali (Louisville); Canadian journalist Peter C. Newman (Vancouver); two network newscasters—CBS anchor Dan Rather (Austin) and ABC anchor Hugh Downs (Phoenix); NBC sportscaster Bob Costas; record-breaking quarterback Steve Young (San Francisco); best-selling mystery author Robert B. Parker (Boston); American Movie Classics host Nick Clooney (Cincinnati); former Texas first lady Nellie Connally (Houston); and former New York City Mayor Ed Koch (New York).

To maintain hands-on quality in all of its periodicals and books, Towery has long used the latest production methods available. The company was the first production environment in the United States to combine desktop publishing with color separations and image scanning to produce finished film suitable for burning plates for four-color printing. Today, Towery relies on state-of-the-art digital prepress services to produce more than 8,000 pages each year, containing well over 30,000 high-quality color images.

An Internet Pioneer

By combining its long-standing expertise in community-oriented published materials with advanced production capabilities, a global sales force, and extensive data management capabilities, Towery has emerged as a significant provider of Internet-based city information. In keeping with its overall focus on community resources, the company's Internet efforts represent a natural step in the evolution of the business.

The primary product lines within the Internet division are the introCity™ sites. Towery's introCity sites introduce newcomers, visitors, and longtime residents to every facet of a particular community, while

Towery Publishing President and CEO J. Robert Towery has expanded the business his parents started in the 1930s to include a growing array of traditional and electronic published materials, as well as Internet and multimedia services, that are marketed locally, nationally, and internationally.

simultaneously placing the local chamber of commerce at the forefront of the city's Internet activity. The sites include newcomer information, calendars, photos, citywide business listings with everything from nightlife to shopping to family fun, and on-line maps pinpointing the exact location of businesses, schools, attractions, and much more.

Decades of Publishing Expertise

In 1972, current President and CEO J. Robert Towery succeeded his parents in managing the printing and publishing business they had founded nearly four decades earlier. Soon thereafter, he expanded the scope of the company's published materials to include *Memphis* magazine and other successful regional and national publications. In 1985, after selling its locally focused assets, Towery began the trajectory on which it continues today, creating community-oriented materials that are often produced in conjunction with chambers of commerce and other business organizations.

Despite the decades of change, Towery himself follows a long-standing family philosophy of unmatched service and unflinching quality. That approach extends throughout the entire organization to include more than 120 employees at the Memphis headquarters, another 80 located in Northern Kentucky outside Cincinnati, and more than 40 sales, marketing, and editorial staff traveling to and working in a growing list of client cities. All of

its products, and more information about the company, are featured on the Internet at www.towery.com.

In summing up his company's steady growth, Towery restates the essential formula that has driven the business since its first pages

were published: "The creative energies of our staff drive us toward innovation and invention. Our people make the highest possible demands on themselves, so I know that our future is secure if the ingredients for success remain a focus on service and quality."

Towery Publishing was the first production environment in the United States to combine desktop publishing with color separations and image scanning to produce finished film suitable for burning plates for four-color printing. Today, the company's state-of-the-art network of Macintosh and Windows workstations allows it to produce more than 8,000 pages each year, containing well over 30,000 high-quality color images.

The Towery family's publishing roots can be traced to 1935, when R.W. Towery (far left) began producing a series of community histories in Tennessee, Mississippi, and Texas. Throughout the company's history, the founding family has consistently exhibited a commitment to clarity, precision, innovation, and vision.

Originally headquartered in London, **Allsport** has expanded to include offices in New York and Los Angeles. Its pictures have appeared in every major publication in the world, and the best of its portfolio has been displayed at elite photographic exhibitions at the Royal Photographic Society and the Olympic Museum in Lausanne.

Employed as the photographer for the Archdiocese of Denver, **James Baca** has won numerous awards in *Catholic Press* and *Colorado Press* in the past 20 years. He has photographed for *Ebony*, numerous Catholic magazines, Lakeside Amusement Park, KWGN-TV, the Colorado Mining Association, and other organizations.

Originally from Springfield, Missouri, **Robert Bridges** specializes in landscape, garden, and macrophotography. A self-employed photographer, he has been represented by Garden Image Stock and has contributed images to such organizations as Frontier Airlines and Adventure Media.

Jan Butchofsky-Houser specializes in travel photography and has coauthored the third edition of a travel guidebook, *Hidden Mexico*. Her photos have appeared in dozens of magazines, newspapers, books, advertisements, and brochures, as well as on video and album covers. She has served as an editorial/research associate for the Berkeley, California-based Ulysses Press and currently manages Dave G.

© ERIC WUNROW

Houser Stock Photography. Her honors include two Bronze awards from the Society of American Travel Writers (SATW).

Owner of Cuerden Advertising Design, **Glenn Cuerden** has had photos in several books on Colorado history, and specializes in corporate, architectural, editorial, illustrative, and digital photography. He has participated in several photography benefits over the past 20 years, as well as a number of one-man exhibitions and group/juried photo exhibitions.

Lee Foster, a veteran travel writer and photographer, has had his work published in major travel magazines and newspapers. He maintains a stock library that features images of more than 250 destinations around the world.

◄ A native of Phoenix, Arizona, **Brian Gadbery** specializes in journalism, people, and travel photography. His images have been included in *USA Today*, and his awards include first place in the 1988 Poy Sports Feature Photo contest.

Specializing in travel, nature, landscape, fine art, and commercial photography, **Catherine Gehm** has had her photographs published through Ariel Books, Random House, and McGraw-Hill.

Originally from Denver, **Blaine Harrington III** has traveled around the globe, visiting nine countries in the past year. He is a regular contributor to Insight Guides, Fodor's, Travel Holiday, and Avalanche calendars, and has worked on book assignments for the National Geographic Society and Time-Life. His photographs have appeared in several Towery publications.

A contributing editor to *Vacations* and *Cruises & Tours* magazines, and coauthor of the travel guidebook *Hidden Coast of California*, **Dave G. Houser** specializes in cruise/luxury travel,

personality, health, and history photography. He has been a runner-up for the Lowell Thomas Travel Journalist of the Year Award and was named the 1984 Society of American Travel Writers' Photographer of the Year.

Kieffer Nature Stock was started in 1986 and represents the work of John Kieffer and other photographers. The company specializes in the landscapes of the American West and has had work published by organizations such as McGraw-Hill, Delta Airlines, and Ogilvy & Mather, as well as in magazines such as *Time*, *Backpacker*, *Reader's Digest*, *Smithsonian*, and *Runner's World*.

Employed by Stretch Photography, **Charles W. Ledford** has photographed people in 35 states and in 45 countries around the world.

Mark and **Jennifer Miller** are the owners and operators of Mark & Jennifer Miller Photos. Published in *Field & Stream*, *Country Journal*, *Outdoor Life*, and *Backpacker*, among others, the Millers specialize in nature, wildlife, and national parks photography.

Self-employed as a freelance photographer, **Tom O'Hara** specializes in urban, portrait, black-and-white, and travel photography. He has worked in the Denver area for more than 25 years.

Photophile, established in San Diego in 1967, has more than 1 million color images on file, culled from more than 85 contributing local and international photographers. Subjects range from images of Southern California to adventure, sports, wildlife and underwater scenes, business, industry, people, science and research, health and medicine, and travel photography. Included on Photophile's client list are American Express, *Guest Informant*, and Franklin Stoorza.

Specializing in travel stock photography, **Brett Shoaf** owns Artistic Visuals, and has photographed images for companies such as Road Runner Card Co., Legoland California, and AAA. He has contributed images to the *San Diegan Guide* and several other Towery publications.

A freelance photographer with more than 17 years of experience, **Dan Tye** has traveled across the United States to photograph wildlife. He specializes in landscapes and nature scenes, and many of his photographs focus on regional points of interest in the Midwest.

Originally from Wisconsin, **Eric Wunrow** specializes in photography and graphic design. His images have sold worldwide in publishing and advertising media, often including text and graphics or illustrations of his own design.

For further information about the photographers appearing in *Denver: On Top of the World*, please contact Towery Publishing.

Library of Congress Cataloging-in-Publication Data

Smythe, Pete, 1911-
   Denver : on top of the world / introduction by Pete Smythe ; art direction by Brian Groppe.
      p. cm. — (Urban tapestry series)
   Includes index.
   ISBN 1-881096-86-6 (alk. paper)
      1. Denver (Colo.)—Civilization.   2. Denver (Colo.)—Pictorial works.   3. Denver
(Colo.)—Economic conditions.   4. Business enterprises—Colorado—Denver.   I. Groppe,
Brian. II. Title. III. Series.

   F784.D45 S69 2001
   978.8'83—dc21

                                                                            00-067623

© TOM O'HARA

Printed in China

Towery Publishing, Inc., The Towery Building, 1835 Union Avenue, Memphis, TN 38104
WWW.TOWERY.COM

Publisher: J. Robert Towery **Executive Publisher**: Jenny McDowell **National Sales
Manager**: Stephen Hung **Marketing Director**: Carol Culpepper **Project Directors**:
Danna Clark, Nancy Kemp Crego, Andrea Glazier, Linda Sorrento **Executive Editor**: David B.
Dawson **Managing Editor**: Lynn Conlee **Senior Editors**: Carlisle Hacker, Brian L. Johnston
Editors: Jay Adkins, Stephen M. Deusner, Rebecca E. Farabough, Danna M. Greenfield, Ginny
Reeves, Sabrina Schroeder **Profile Writer**: Lynn Bronikowski **Photography Editor**:
Jonathan Postal **Photographic Consultant**: Frank Varney **Profile Designers**: Rebekah
Barnhardt, Laurie Beck, Glen Marshall **Production Manager**: Brenda Pattat **Photography
Coordinator**: Robin Lankford **Production Assistants**: Robert Barnett, Loretta Lane, Robert
Parrish **Digital Color Supervisor**: Darin Ipema **Digital Color Technicians**: Eric Friedl,
Brent Salazar, Mark Svetz **Digital Scanning Technicians**: Zac Ives, Brad Long **Production
Resources Manager**: Dave Dunlap Jr. **Print Coordinator**: Beverly Timmons

Index of Profiles

Alpine Lumber Company 190

Aspen Petroleum Products 242

Aurora Public Schools 169

CIBER Inc. 216

Clear Channel Colorado 244

Colorado Heart Imaging 240

Colorado Office of Economic Development and International Trade 212

Community Colleges of Colorado 192

Denver Broncos Football Club 186

Denver Business Journal 182

Denver Rocky Mountain News 170

Durrant 202

Foster and Son 183

Freeman Group Public Relations 222

The Gates Rubber Company 172

HenryGill Advertising 204

Insurance Design & Placement, Inc. 224

KeyBank/McDonald Investments Inc. 226

Kimsey Electrical Contracting 234

Kodak Colorado 194

Level 3 Communications, Inc. 243

Lucent Technologies NetworkCare Knowledge Center 236

Marriott 196

McGuckin Hardware 184

Merrill Lynch & Company 174

Pacific Western Technologies, Ltd. 214

PEAK Resources Inc. 217

People's Choice Transportation 193

The Phil Long Dealerships 180

PorterCare Adventist Health 176

ProLogis 220

Radisson Stapleton Plaza 200

Rocky Mountain Orthodontics 178

S. A. Miro, Inc. 206

SUPERVALU Inc. 238

Towery Publishing, Inc. 250

TRW Inc. 208

Univision 50/KCEC-TV 218

Xilinx Colorado 232